Iryna Kravchenko

The Role of Bishops in Icelandic Society (1056–1211)

Iryna Kravchenko

The Role of Bishops in Icelandic Society (1056–1211)

Political and Social Aspects of Activities

VDM Verlag Dr. Müller

Impressum/Imprint (nur für Deutschland/ only for Germany)
Bibliografische Information der Deutschen Nationalbibliothek: Die Deutsche Nationalbibliothek verzeichnet diese Publikation in der Deutschen Nationalbibliografie; detaillierte bibliografische Daten sind im Internet über http://dnb.d-nb.de abrufbar.
Alle in diesem Buch genannten Marken und Produktnamen unterliegen warenzeichen-, marken- oder patentrechtlichem Schutz bzw. sind Warenzeichen oder eingetragene Warenzeichen der jeweiligen Inhaber. Die Wiedergabe von Marken, Produktnamen, Gebrauchsnamen, Handelsnamen, Warenbezeichnungen u.s.w. in diesem Werk berechtigt auch ohne besondere Kennzeichnung nicht zu der Annahme, dass solche Namen im Sinne der Warenzeichen- und Markenschutzgesetzgebung als frei zu betrachten wären und daher von jedermann benutzt werden dürften.

Coverbild: www.purestockx.com

Verlag: VDM Verlag Dr. Müller Aktiengesellschaft & Co. KG
Dudweiler Landstr. 99, 66123 Saarbrücken, Deutschland
Telefon +49 681 9100-698, Telefax +49 681 9100-988, Email: info@vdm-verlag.de

Herstellung in Deutschland:
Schaltungsdienst Lange o.H.G., Berlin
Books on Demand GmbH, Norderstedt
Reha GmbH, Saarbrücken
Amazon Distribution GmbH, Leipzig
ISBN: 978-3-639-10688-6

Imprint (only for USA, GB)
Bibliographic information published by the Deutsche Nationalbibliothek: The Deutsche Nationalbibliothek lists this publication in the Deutsche Nationalbibliografie; detailed bibliographic data are available in the Internet at http://dnb.d-nb.de.
Any brand names and product names mentioned in this book are subject to trademark, brand or patent protection and are trademarks or registered trademarks of their respective holders. The use of brand names, product names, common names, trade names, product descriptions etc. even without a particular marking in this works is in no way to be construed to mean that such names may be regarded as unrestricted in respect of trademark and brand protection legislation and could thus be used by anyone.

Cover image: www.purestockx.com

Publisher:
VDM Verlag Dr. Müller Aktiengesellschaft & Co. KG
Dudweiler Landstr. 99, 66123 Saarbrücken, Germany
Phone +49 681 9100-698, Fax +49 681 9100-988, Email: info@vdm-verlag.de

Copyright © 2009 by the author and VDM Verlag Dr. Müller Aktiengesellschaft & Co. KG and licensors
All rights reserved. Saarbrücken 2009

Printed in the U.S.A.
Printed in the U.K. by (see last page)
ISBN: 978-3-639-10688-6

Table of contents:

Table of contents: 1
Preface 2
Introduction 3
Historical Introduction 8
Chapter 1. The Foundation of Bishops' Authority 11
    a) Family background 11
    b) Election and consecration 20
Chapter 2. Conflicts 27
    a) Partaking in conflicts caused by others 28
    b) Causing conflicts 41
Chapter 3. Other tasks 47
    a) Lawmaking 48
    b) Education 51
Chapter 4. Icelandic pattern of bishop's office in European context 55
    a) Duties of bishop according to Christian regulations 55
    b) Bishop's office in Germany, Denmark, Norway 57
    c) Influence of Gregorian reform on Iceland 60
Conclusion: 65
Abbreviations: 71
Appendices: 72
    Appendix 1: Genealogical tables 72
    Appendix 2: Lists of ecclesiastical succession 76
Bibliography: 79

Preface

This book is largely based on my Master Dissertation which I wrote at the University of Oslo from 2004 to 2006 under the supervision of Professor Jón Viðar Sigurðsson. In the following years I have continued to work on the subject and have updated some of my conclusions.

My object here is history; it might have been theology, but it is not. The focus rests upon political and social issues in Icelandic society. A great deal of general information about the period in both Iceland and neighbouring countries is skipped in this book. The best introduction to the history, economy, political and social institutions of the period remains "History of the Icelandic Commonwealth" by Jón Jóhannesson. Solid overviews over Scandinavian history are presented in "Medieval Scandinavia: An Encyclopedia". I also hope that the reader will forgive me my dry "telegraphic" style.

I am indebted to many people for the successful completion of this work. First, I would like to thank my supervisor Jón Viðar Sigurðsson, who had the kindness to share his vast knowledge in the field of Icelandic political history. I have benefited a great deal from Timothy A. Bolton and Joanna A. Skórzewska for much useful advice and valuable discussions. All my teachers and colleagues deserve my gratitude for offering me both their friendship and their professional help.

I would also like to thank Maria Kimasheva, Kirsten Trued and John Carragee for helping me with the technical side of my work.

Introduction

Historical development of one of Europe's geographic margins – the Icelandic Commonwealth – deserves particular attention in modern medieval scholarship. This island, situated in the north-eastern corner of the Atlantic Sea, escaped foreign invasion, quick social, political, and economic changes, and religious wars. No doubt, Christianization, cultural and intellectual influences from Europe made a certain impact on Icelandic mentality and way of living, but Iceland nevertheless retained its traditional law, culture, and social structure relatively intact throughout the transition. Among all institutions of medieval Iceland, the Church was the only one built on a European model. Although prestigious, the Church wielded little power of its own; although wealthy, its influence was borrowed from positions in the political realm. The heads of the Icelandic Church evoke a deep interest for historians. Who were these people standing between claims of the ecclesiastical order and the actual life of their country, between European and Icelandic cultural and socio-political realities?

The main question I intend to discuss in this study concerns the roles of bishops in Icelandic society from the middle of the eleventh century (1056) to the beginning of the thirteenth century (1211). The time span under consideration has been dictated by two factors: the foundation of the Episcopal office in Iceland and significant change of the political situation at the beginning of the thirteenth century.

Considering the extensiveness of the question, the study is divided into four main parts.

The first chapter examines the bishops' backgrounds. The general question here is – who became a bishop? What was the bishops' network and how did it influence them? Could a bishop strengthen his position; if so, by what means? Another dimension of this issue is to understand those who were behind the scenes. Who was interested in promoting the candidate for the episcopacy? Did this pattern change during the period?

The second chapter defines the particular political phenomenon of conflicts in Iceland and addresses the role of the bishops role in these conflicts. Conflicts that arose in Iceland from the end of the twelfth century through the first half of the thirteenth century were the central theme of the contemporary sagas (*samtíðasögur*). In one sense, the attention of such prominent sources influences our comprehension of this topic, but in another sense it highlights the importance of conflicts in the political life of the country, especially in the first half of the thirteenth century. As the main field of political rivalry, conflicts were the surest means to power and prestige in Icelandic society. The principal participants were the chieftains, but they also could be bishops and farmers. Was there any difference between the bishops and the chieftains in conflicts? It is interesting also to see how bishops' backgrounds mirrored their mode of participation in conflicts.

Two important aspects of bishops' activities – lawmaking and education – are discussed in the third chapter. Knowledge of laws was highly appreciated in Iceland. The legislative function of the

Law Council gave the chieftains prestige and status. Bishops were also known for the making of laws. What was their role in the country's lawmaking process? Education played a significant role in self-awareness of elite circles. Knowledgeable people were much respected in Icelandic society. Two schools under the patronage of bishops to have existed – at Skálholt and at Hólar. What was the place of bishops in the educational process?

Finally, chapter four analyzes the functions of the Icelandic bishops in the European context. The characteristics of the Icelandic bishop's office will be compared with the prescribed duties and authority of the high ecclesiastics according to Church regulations as well as to actual practice in Norway, Denmark, and Germany, which were culturally and ecclesiastically connected to Iceland.

Another aspect under consideration is episcopal relationships with other ecclesiastical authorities. In addition to membership in elite Icelandic political and social circles, bishops were also an important part of the Christian hierarchy. The study examines relationships between two Icelandic bishoprics and the archdiocese to which they belonged during the Commonwealth period. The substance, rationale, and outcome of archdiocesan policy towards Iceland are examined.

This thesis considers the following bishops: of Skálholt bishopric – Ísleifr Gizurarson (1056–80), Gizurr Ísleifsson (1082–1118), Þorlákr Runólfsson (1118–33), Magnús Einarsson (1134–48), Hallr Teitsson (d. 1148), Klængr Þorsteinsson (1152–76), Þorlákr Þórhallsson (1178–93), Páll Jónsson (1195–1211); of Hólar bishopric – Jón Ögmundsson (1106–1121), Ketill Þorsteinsson (1122–45), Björn Gilsson (1147–62), Brandr Sæmundsson (1163–1201).

Spelling of the Icelandic names follows Old Norse; spelling of all other names follows modern English. All translations of texts from *Biskupa sögur*, if not separately noted, are mine.

Appendix 1 deals with the family connections of the bishops. Appendix 2 covers a) ecclesiastical succession of Icelandic bishops during the period studied; b) ecclesiastical succession of archbishops in the three archdiocese to which Iceland belonged; and c) papal succession in the Catholic Church.

As a phenomenon, the bishops' role in Icelandic society has never been fully analysed by scholars. Scholarly works on bishops mostly concern bishops' biographies and only blankly repeat accounts from the sources.[1] Although there are several studies which briefly review the bishops participation in conflicts[2], the area of bishops' involvement in the conflicts has not gained much attention from scholars. For example, Jón Viðar Sigurðsson in his *Chieftains and power in the Icelandic commonwealth* says a few words about the bishops' participation in conlicts and their involvement in mediation.[3]

---

[1] Jón Helgason 1925; Magnús Már Lárusson 1965; Sigurður Nordal1990; Jón Jóhannesson 1974
[2] Byock 1982; Byock1988; Miller1990
[3] Jón Viðar Sigurðsson 1999

The most recent research on Christianity in Iceland and bishops as a part of the social system was published by Órri Vésteinsson.[4] He mainly discusses bishops' family backgrounds and involvement in secular politics. However, his research is structured as a biographical study and does not detail bishops' tasks.

My aim in this study is to examine bishops as a part of the social network in Iceland. I analyse the bishops' role in conflicts, lawmaking, and education; in addition, I explore the mechanism of the bishops' influence and the background to their politics. It is also necessary to define the influence of episcopal politics and the Roman Church movements, such as the Gregorian reform, on Icelandic ecclesiastics.

Since there is no focused research on the bishop's role in Icelandic society, my study is mainly source based. Three categories of written sources have been taken into consideration at particular stages of my research. These are contemporary narrative sources, documentary evidence, and laws. However, my research is for the most based on contemporary narrative sources – *Sturlunga saga* and *Biskupa sögur*. These sources are thoroughly analysed from the historical and literary points of view. Contemporary sagas are generally considered as reliable evidence as the distance between the events they describe and the time when they were written down is about 20–70 years.[55]

Sturlunga saga[6], ca. 1300, is a large collection of sagas by various authors and spanning events from 1117 (in *Þorgils saga ok Hafliða*) to ca. 1265 (*Sturlu þáttr*). There are two vellum manuscripts: Króksfjarðarbók (I) (AM. 122A fol.) and Reykjafjarðarbók (II) (AM. 122B fol.). The former was probably written in the middle of the fourteenth century. The latter manuscript dates back to the end of the fourteenth century. Neither II nor I is the original. The most probable candidate for the compiler of the *Sturlunga saga* collection was Þórðr Narfason the Lawman, one of the three sons of a priest, Narfi Snorrasson (1237–87).

In my study, I focus on *the Þorgils saga ok Hafliða, Hvamm-Sturla saga, Guðmundar saga dýra, Guðmund saga biskups, Haukadæla þáttr, Íslendingasaga*. The main emphasis is laid upon *Þorgils saga ok Hafliða* and *Hvamm-Sturla saga* as they contain information about bishops' participation in the conflicts.

Biskupa sögur[7] are stories about Icelandic bishops of the two sees of Skálholt and Hólar from the eleventh to the fourteenth centuries. As a source, the *Biskupa sögur* are situated between saga,

---

[4] Órri Vésteinsson 1996
[5] Jón Viðar Sigurðsson 1999: 18
[6] The information about *Sturlunga saga* is based on: Thomas, R.G. "Introduction" of *Sturlunga saga* I. Trans. Julia H. McGrew. New York. 1970, 13–45; Zimmerling, A. V. "Introduction" of Sturla Þórðarson. Íslendingasaga. Trans. Zimmerling, A. Sankt-Petersburg. 2007, 9–64
[7] The general information about *Hungrvaka, Þorláks saga A, Þorláks saga B, Páls saga* is based on: Jónas Kristjánsson. Eddas and Sagas. Icelandic medieval literature. Reykjavík. 1997, 181–4. G. Vigfusson and F. Y. Powell. Origines Islandicae: a collection of the more important sagas and other native writings relating to the

saint's lives and ecclesiastical history. There is a tendency to divide *Biskupa sögur* into two categories: saints' lives (the sagas about Þorlákr and Jón) and "historical" works. However, many of the "historical" sagas, which could be considered historical works, are influenced in style and structure by the hagiographies.[8]

The five first bishops of Skálholt are commemorated in *Hungrvaka* (literally "Appetiser"). *Hungrvaka* can be dated within rather narrow limits – after 1206 but before 1211. The saga is generally considered to be the work of one man. The author used *Íslendingabók* and a number of other written sources, including documents no longer extant, and in the manner of Ari the Wise he also refers to the testimony of specific individuals. The conclusion of the book shows that it was written as an introduction to *Þorláks saga,* which was probably newly finished at that time. The text of *Hungrvaka* is based on a single lost vellum manuscript, of which there is no provenance until after 1601. There are three main complete manuscripts, which trace back to the lost copy: AM. 379, 1654; AM. 205, J.G. 1643; AM. 380, vellum, 1643; and several extracts and abstracts.[9]

Jóns saga[10] is not known in Latin but in three variant Icelandic versions (principal texts AM. 234 fol. (c.1340), Stock. perg. fol. nr. 5 (c. 1360). *Version A* or *Saga Jóns biskups his elzta* was written by an unknown author around 1200. It is most likely that an older version was ordered by Bishop Brandr Sæmundson of Hólar; later, Brand's successor, Bishop Guðmundr Arason (1161–1237) sent it to a monk of the monastery Þingeyrar – Gunnlaugr Leifsson (d. 1218/19), who, on the basis of this text wrote a Latin life of St. Jón – *Jóns biskups saga eptir Gunnlaug múnk*. This text has not been preserved. What now exist is the Old Norse translation of Gunnlaugr work, written most probably after 1250, but not later than the beginning of the fourteenth century. *Jónssaga hin yngsta* or *Version C* follows the Gunnlaug version. However, Margaret Cormack in her "Introduction" to the English translation of the *Jóns saga* points out that the oldest version of the saga is based on Gunnlaug's Latin text.[11]

The three versions of the *Þorláks saga* have not been the subject of a detailed philological study and their relationship is therefore still ambiguous. *Version A* is a true contemporary saga, written in Latin perhaps ten years after the bishop's death. The saga can be counted as a comparatively reliable historical source despite its hagiographic nature.[12] The account is written as the typical *vita* of the holy man with little attention paid to his involvement in secular affairs. The preserved manuscript

---

settlement and early history of Iceland. Oxford. 1905, 420–4, 567–8. Schach, P. *Icelandic sagas*. Boston. 1984, 63–9
[8] Ásdís Egilsdóttir 1992: 207–20
[9] Ásdís Egilsdóttir. "Formáli" of *Biskupa sögur* II. Reykjavík 2000, vi - xxxi.
[10] The information about *Jóns saga* is based on *Formáli* to *Biskupa sögur* I. Gefnar út af Hinu Islenzka Bókmentafèlagi. Kbhvn. 1858, xxxviii - xlii.
[11] Cormack, M. "Introduction" of *Saga of bishop Jón of Hólar* / Medieval hagiography: an anthology. Ed. T. Head. Trans. by. M. Cormack. New York 2001, 595–9
[12] Jónas Kristjánsson 1997: 181

(Stockh. perg. fol. No. 5) is dated 1360. There is a fragment of *A-version* (AM 383 4to I) called *D-version*. Version B or *Oddaverja-þáttr* (AM. 382) was written in Old Norse in the middle or latter half of the thirteenth century by an unknown author. He took *Þorláks saga A* and put a new prologue at its head, and then inserted into the body of the text stories about the dispute over benefices (*staðarmál*) and the other matters of contention between the bishop and Jón Loptsson. The saga might have been created as a propaganda tool during the episcopacy of Bishop Árni Þorláksson who also had conflicts with chieftains over *staðarmál*.[13] *C-version* is preserved in seven manuscripts that date from the fourteenth to seventeenth century. This text fills gaps of the badly preserved *B-version*.

Páls saga was compiled shortly after the bishop's death (1211) and is an even more personal biography than *Þorláks saga*. It is also remarkably free of the Biblical quotations and Latinisms that abound in the biographies of Jón and Þorlákr. G. Vigfusson considers *Páls saga* as a part of the trilogy that also includes *Hungrvaka* and *Þorláks saga*.[14]

Working on *Biskupa sögur* I used original documents and translations by G. Vigfusson and F. Y. Powell in *Origines Islandicae* and by M. Cormack in *Medieval hagiography: an anthology*.

Letters and documents from *Diplomatarium Islandicum* and *Diplomatarium Norvegicum* enrich the present study with information about the relations between Icelandic and Norwegian secular and ecclesiastical elites.

The collection of Icelandic laws is known as *Grágás*. There are two main manuscripts – *Konungsbók* and *Staðarhóldsbók* – which were written down in the middle of thirteenth century and around 1270 respectively.[15] The Code of Christian Law forms the first chapter of *Grágás*. In the diocese of Skálholt the Code remained in force until 1275, when the Code of Christian Law of Bishop Árni Þorláksson (*Kristiréttur Árna biskups*) was adopted. Nevertheless, in the diocese of Hólar it was abrogated by royal decree on October 19, 1354.[16] From 1275, ecclesiastical laws were separated from the secular law codex *Grágás* and this acceptance and separation established canon law in Iceland. *Grágás* did not, however, constitute an officially promulgated legal code since the law manuscripts were private law books.

---

[13] Órri Vésteinsson 2000: 115
[14] Vigfusson 1905: 421
[15] Grágás, p. 1–21
[16] Ibid.

Historical Introduction

The present review is intended to provide readers unfamiliar with Icelandic ecclesiastical history some background.

The first human inhabitants of the island were Irish hermits, who most likely left it soon after the arrival of the first colonists of Scandinavian origin in the ninth century. Most of the new immigrants were pagans; however, several families and individuals who settled first in the British Isles or the North Sea islands were baptized or took prime-signing (*lat. primo signatio*, Old Norse *prímsignan*).[17]

The end of the tenth century in Iceland was marked by arrival of several Christian missions. The first missionary, Friðrekr, was an envoy of the Hamburg-Bremen archdiocese to which Iceland formally belonged. He converted some chieftains, but had to leave the island. More active and successful in promoting Christianity in Iceland were Norwegians kings. Another German by origin – Þangbrandr – was a missionary sent by the Norwegian king, Olaf Tryggvasson (995–1000). Þrangbrandr managed to baptize several chieftains: Hallr of Siða, Hjalti Skeggjason, and Gizurr the White. Gizurr was a father of the first bishop of Iceland – Ísleifr. In the sagas, Olaf Tryggvasson is described as a king anxious to promote Christianity in his own country and in other places of interest. Under certain circumstances, Icelanders agreed to accept baptism and become Christians. This decision was announced at the General Assembly (*alþingi*) in 999 or 1000. No permanent see was established at that time.

During the eleventh century, Iceland was visited by missionary bishops of English, Irish and German origin. King Olav Haraldsson (1015–28, d. 1030) seems to have sent Bishop Bernhard Vilráðsson to Iceland. Following Bishop Bernhard came several of his colleagues. Bishop Kolr is said to have been in Iceland for only few years; he stayed with Hallr Þórarinsson at Haukdælir. Kolr died in Iceland and became the first bishop to be buried at Skálholt. Interestingly, this Hallr became a foster father of two future bishops: Bishop of Skálholt Þorlákr Runólfsson and Bishop of Hólar Björn Gilsson. Hallr also fostered and educated Teitr – a son of Bishop Ísleifr – and Teitr's son and a future bishop-elect Hallr. There was also a mission of three Armenians, Petrus, Abraham, Stephanus, who were not much welcomed on the island.

Missionary bishops laid down the basis of the Christian organization and learning in Iceland. The Haukdælir family, which had close contact with the missionaries, established and controlled the chief positions of the Christian institutions of Iceland.

---

[17] a religious act, preliminary to christening; persons thus signed with the cross were catechumens, and if adults they could join in the social life among Christians; they were also admitted to a special part of the mass (primsigndra messa = *the mass for the 'prime-signed'*), whereas all intercourse with heathens was forbidden. An infant who died, having received the prima signatio, but not baptism, was to be buried in the outskirts of the churchyard, where the consecrated and unconsecrated earth meet, and without burial service. Sourse: An Icelandic-English dictionary by Cleasby and Vigfusson, 1874

The first native bishop in Iceland was Ísleifr Gizuzarson, who held office from 1056 to 1080. Regarding the foundation of a fixed see, the "real" situation is hard to determine; there is not enough data for it. According to *Hungrvaka*, Icelanders asked Ísleifr to become their bishop "because of his learning and reputation."[18] However, it seems likely that this putative popular call was, in fact, the initiative of the Haukdælir family to establish the office and become the single ecclesiastical authority in Iceland. The see was founded at the family estate of Haukdælir – Skálholt. Strictly speaking, Ísleifr was also a missionary bishop who had a permanent residence in Iceland – a farm at Skálholt. This farm and a church were apparently established by Ísleif's father, chieftain Gizurr the White[19]. Most probably there was a rivalry between the envoys from European archdioceses and Ísleifr with the result that Archbishop Adalbert forbade Icelanders to receive service from missionary bishops, and after 1080, there were no foreign bishops in Iceland.[20]

Organization of Skálholt as the Church institution was established by Ísleif's son and successor – Gizurr (1082–1118). He donated his family estate as the episcopal see and introduced the payment of tithes. Moreover, Gizurr had a hand in the foundation of the second bishopric in Iceland, at Hólar. Sources – *Hungrvaka* and *Saga Jóns biskups his elzta* – agree in the description of the foundation of the second bishopric. According to the Saga: "Northerners asked Bishop Gizurr to establish a bishopric in the Northern Quarter, because…their Quarter was the most populous and the largest, and therefore had the greatest need of Episcopal visitation."[21] Gizurr named the most distinguished candidate – Jón Ögmundarson. Hjalti Hugason is right in stating that the foundation of the see at Hólar from Skálholt would be an embodiment of the political competition between the southern and northern bishoprics at the end of the twelfth and the beginning of the thirteenth century.[22]

On the other hand, Jón's family relations, indicate continuing close connections with the holders of the southern see. Jón was a foster son of the Haukdælir and so, the family could influence him. The most likely reason for the foundation of the second bishopric was to try to establish the control of the Haukdælir family over the northern territories. "Afterwards many meetings were held about the matter, and it was decided that the see of the bishop of the Northerners would be established up north in Hjaltadalr, on the estate called Hólar. A distinguished priest called Illugi lived there; of the noble men of the Northern Quarter only he was prepared to depart from his patrimony for the sake of God and needs of Holy Church. Previously there had been long arguments among the chieftains as to who should depart from his patrimony."[23]

---

[18] Hungrvaka, 2
[19] Hungrvaka, 2; Hörður Áugústsson 1990: 299
[20] Hungrvaka, 2
[21] *Jóns saga helga*, 7. Forward: Jsh. Trans. by M.Cormack. Her translation follows *Saga Jóns biskups his elzta* in the edition of *Biskupa sögur* by Guðbrandur Vigfússon. Copenhagen, 1858
[22] Hjalti Hugason 2000: 131
[23] Jsh, 7

Ecclesiastically, from the very foundation of the first bishopric Iceland was a part of the diocese of Hamburg-Bremen. Authority of Hamburg-Bremen over churches in Sweden, Denmark, Norway, Iceland, Greenland, and certain *Scridenium* was affirmed by Pope Victor II (1055–7).[24] At the end of the eleventh century, the growing tension between Danish kings and German emperors made the subordination of the Danish bishops under the archbishop of Hamburg-Bremen intolerable. The new archbishopric was founded at Lund in 1104 as the metropolitan centre originally for all Scandinavia. The next era in development of Icelandic church started from the foundation of archbishopric at Nidaros (Norway) in 1154. The Nidaros period is very crucial for the development of the Icelandic church. It accompanied the growing authority of the papacy, changes in relationships between the Church and the Crown in Norway and increasing interest of Norway into Icelandic affairs.

---

[24] Diplomatarium Islandicum, no. 19. Forward: DI

Chapter 1. The Foundation of Bishops' Authority

This chapter considers the beginnings of the bishops' careers. Particularly, it attempts to display: a) their family backgrounds; and b) the election and consecration processes. As among other peoples, the family was the most basic building block of Icelandic social and political organization. The sagas give a great attention to the ancestors, family members, close and distant relatives and friends of their heroes. All these connections form a network of kingship groups, which have their own place and function in the social hierarchy. In the search for the basis of bishops' power the important issue is to examine the position of the families which normally offered their members as candidates for the sees. The top of the political and social hierarchy was occupied by those chieftains who possessed a chieftaincy (goðorð). Did the families mentioned above possess a chieftaincy? The matter of interest in the present chapter is also the bishops' relationships with the most powerful families.

The second part of the chapter deals with the process of election and consecration. Medieval Church developed an elaborate system of ecclesiastical elections based on democratic principle.[25] In spite of this, the selection of high ecclesiastics in Europe was often accompanied by considerable political machinations. These maneuverings underlined the political, economic, and governmental importance of the Church in Europe. What was the pattern of election and consecration in Iceland? Were the elections a significant political event?

a) Family background

Skálholt bishopric
The first Icelandic bishop, Ísleifr Gizurarson (1056–1080), belonged to one of the most powerful and influential families of Iceland – to the Haukdælir – and possessed a *goðorð*.
In *Hungrvaka*[26] a progenitor of the family is called Ketilbjörn the Old from Mosfell which is in the southwest. One of his sons – Teitr – founded an estate at Skálholt. His son – chieftain Gizurr the White – played the leading role in bringing about the adoption the Christianity by law in Iceland. Gizurr married Þórdís, a sister of the Lawspeaker Skapti Þóroddson and daughter of Þóroddr goði. One of their sons was Ísleifr.[27] Ísleifr's uncle – Skapti, the son of chieftain Þóroddr from Hjalli in the Ölfus district, was a lawspeaker for twenty-seven summers (1004–30), longer than any other man. Scholars consider Skapti's contribution to the legislation system of Iceland – he established the law of the Fifth Court – as having marked the beginning of a new epoch in the history of the Icelandic nation.[28] Through Skapti Ísleifr's family intermarried with high-powered kin at Eyjafjörður on the North.

---

[25] Mulen 2002: 175–6
[26] Hungrvaka, 2
[27] see appendix 1A
[28] Jón Jóhannesson 1974: 70

Skapti's son Þorsteinn Holmunnr married Jódís, a daughter of Guðmundr the Powerful of Möðruvellir in Eyjafjörður. Guðmundr is the only clear example from the early part of the Commonwealth period of a chieftain having accumulated power beyond ordinary limits. He was only man of his time to earn himself the epithet *hinn ríki*.[29]

Ísleifr's family acquired great wealth that made it possible for him to study abroad at the monastery of Herford in Germany.[30] The abbess of the monastery – Godesthi – was the aunt of Duke Ordulfr; the Duke was married to Úlfhildr, the daughter of St. Olav, the King of Norway.[31] There is another connection to St. Olav. One of Ísleifr sons, Teitr, had been adopted by Hallr Þórarinsson hinn mildi in Haukdælir. Hallr had been in Norway and was a retainer of St. Olav.[32]

On return to Iceland Ísleifr acquired Skálholt as his estate and settled down there. Although it is not entirely clear whether it had been his father's main estate. Vésteinsson shows that *Kristini saga* and *Landnámabók* have Gizurr living at Höfði. *Njáls saga* mentions Mosfell as Gizurr's farm.[33] Ísleifr married Dalla, a daughter of Þorvaldr from Ás.[34]

Gizurr Ísleifsson (1082–1118) was one of three sons of Ísleifr and almost certainly not the eldest one.[35] His brother Teitr died before him (d. 1110).[36] Consequently, Gizurr did not inherit his father's estate. Teitr of Haukdælir is more likely than Gizurr to have held the chieftaincy of Mosfellings.[37] From Teitr are descended the people of Haukdælir. Teitr's pupil was Ari Þorgilsson the Learned (1068–1148). Another brother Þorvaldr dwelt at his estate at Hraungerði in the district of Hlói, and, according to *Hungrvaka* was a great chieftain.[38]

Gizurr was married to Steinunn Þorgrimsdottir, a widow of Þórir Skegg-Broddarson of Hof in Vápnafjörðr, who probably held the Hofverja chieftaincy.[39] The fact that Gizurr went to live at his wife's inheritance at Hof in Vápnafjörðr on the East suggests that his brothers Teitr and Þorvaldr had already acquired wealth and power within their family. Most likely, he was the last alive son of Bishop Ísleifr, because during the elections of the next bishop at Alþingi in 1080 there was no other son.

According to *Hungrvaka* and A- and B-versions of *Saga Jóns biskup*, Gizurr was sent by his father to the same monastery in Saxony, Herford to be educated.[40] This is not unlikely, but cause for doubt remains. Closer examination of the sources reveals that both texts, especially redactions of *Saga*

---

[29] Ibid., p. 226
[30] Hungvaka, 2; Jsh, 1
[31] Jón Jóhannesson 1974: 144
[32] Órri Vesteinsson 1996: 145
[33] Ibid., p. 21
[34] Hungrvaka, 2
[35] see appendix 1A
[36] Órri Vesteinsson 1996: 146
[37] Sigurður Nordal 1990: 241
[38] Hungrvaka, 2
[39] Órri Vesteinsson 1996: 140
[40] Jsh, 3; Jóns biskups saga eptir Gunnlaug múnk, 5. Forward: Js Gunnlaug

Jóns biskup, pay great attention to bishops' education and teaching. Knowledge was highly valued in Icelandic society, and so nothing special can be surmised from the reference itself. Yet, the mention of education in combination with some other characteristics of high clerics' in these particular texts makes me suspect other roots of this information. Development of bishops' vitae in Germany presents an interesting picture. A particular image of an ideal cleric represented in German bishops' vitae was based upon the classical and Christian literary-biographical traditions. Stephen Jeager indicates that the values and an ideal type of the court cleric were joined to the chivalric ideal.[41] Appearance or rather beauty, clothing, education, knowledge of music and languages, manners, honourable behaviour, speeches, and virtues were a part of the phenomenon of courtesy. One of the tasks of the phenomenon was to signify the social layer of the nobility and to mark its hierarchy. In addition to education, both sagas of Jón have beauty, music skills, and virtues added to characteristics of their hero. It hard to know for certain whether Gizurr studied at Herford or this incident was an invention of his vita's author. Proceeding from the aforementioned evidence, I incline to the latter.

Before entering an ecclesiastical office, Gizurr became a merchant and often sailed abroad.[42]

After the death of Gizurr Þorlákr Runólfsson (1118–33) became a bishop at Skálholt. His ancestry was respectable. Vésteinsson[43] claims that he was descendant from Ketilbjörn gamli like the Haukdælir and from Ögmundr bíldr like St. Jón, and on his mother's side, he was of the Reynistaðarsmen from the North. More important, however, was the fact that he was the great-nephew of Hallr Þórarinsson, who fostered and educated him in Haukdælir.[44] He was the third cousin of his fellow student and later bishop of Hólar, Björn Gilsson.[45] However, in *Hungrvaka* the line of his ancestors stops with Þorkell skotakolls.[46]

The successor of Bishop Þorlákr at Skálholt was Magnús Einarsson (1134–48). He was Bishop Þorlákr's first cousin once removed. He was a distant relative of the Haukdælir and a descendant of Síðu-Hallr, through a direct line from Síðu-Hallr's eldest son's line. A great-uncle of his mother Þuríð Gilsdottir was Hallr from Haukdælir. His stepmother was Oddný, a daughter of Magnús the priest, a son of Þórdr of Reykjaholt.[47]

The next bishop-elect of Skálaholt was Hallr Teitsson (d. 1148). Hallr's father Teitr was a son of Bishop Ísleifr. Teitr had been adopted by Hallr Þórarinsson hinn mildi in Haukdælir.[48] Hallr was probably childless and Teitr seems to have inherited the land from him. Teitr served as a priest and had

---

[41] Jaeger 1983: 324
[42] Hungrvaka, 2
[43] Órri Vésteinsson 1996: 147
[44] Hungrvaka, 6
[45] see appendix 1C
[46] Ibid.
[47] see appendix 1A, 1D
[48] see appendix 1A

a school where the Icelandic secular and ecclesiastical elite were educated. *Sturlunga saga* mentions that Hallr Teitsson "was a powerful chieftain".[49] Teitr did not become a bishop on the occasion of his death in Trect [Utrecht] before his consecration.

When the news of Hallr's death reached Iceland "it was the selection of everyone who was to decide, under the guidance of Björn, bishop of Hólar" that Klængr Þorsteinsson (1152–76) should be *electus*.[50] His family does not seem to have been influential, although their ancestry was respectable.[51] Klængr is listed among the highborn priests of the north in 1143 – when he probably was a cathedral priest at Hólar – and the author of *Hungrvaka* calls him a northerner. Vésteinsson argues that it was clearly Bishop Björn who brought about Klængr's election to the see of Skálholt.[52] If Haukdælir accepted it, (and they apparently did) Klængr was a convenient candidate for them. He was educated under St. Jón at Hólar, and as a cleric had been living with the bishop of Hólar, Ketill. It is also said that he was a good writer, scholar, and scald. The author underlines that Klængr had powerful friends. Among them was a son of the previous bishop-elect Hallr – Gizurr Hallsson. According to the saga, they met in Europe while Gizurr was coming back from the south, from a trip to Barri and Rome. Klængr himself appointed a successor. The new bishop was an abbot of the monastery at Þykkvabær – Þorlákr Þórhallsson (1178–93).

Þorlákr's saga claims that his parents were "of good family and noble ancestry."[53] It is clear that they were not prosperous and probably not influential either.[54] His father was a merchant and a householder but it seems that he was not successful. When Þorlákr was still young, he and his mother went to Oddi where the priest Eyjólfr Sæmundarson taught him. This suggests that his mother was at least well connected. It appears that his family developed quite close ties with the Oddaverjar; one of his sisters later became a concubine of Jón Loptsson. When he was ordained he became a district priest in a small but profitable ministry, and his saga claims that this revenue made it possible for him to go to Paris and Lincoln. However, it must have been Oddaverjar who paid for his education abroad.[55]

On his return to Iceland, Þorlákr became a district priest at the major church-farm and later convent Kirkjubær in Síða under the priest Bjarnhéðinn Sigurðarson, who was named in the list of the highborn men of 1143.[56] In six years, he became a prior of a new house of canons of Þykkvabær in Álftaver from where he progressed to become bishop of Skálholt. At the Alþingi of 1174 there were three candidates. Bishop Klængr chose Þorlákr. The family of Oddaverjar became more powerful and

---

[49] Haukadæla þáttr, 4. Hallr's son Gizurr became the Lawspesker (1181–1200). Gizurr visited Rome and wrote a book *Flos peregrinationis* about Saxony and Germany.
[50] Hungrvaka, 8
[51] see appendix 1D
[52] Órri Vésteinsson 1996: 151
[53] Þorláks saga A, 2. Forward: Þs A
[54] see appendix 1B
[55] Órri Vésteinsson 1996: 152
[56] DI, no. 29

started to compete with the Haukdælir. They could not hope to oust the Haukdælir from Skálholt but could attempt to get some influence through Þorlákr. Therefore, his candidacy was a compromise between two powerful families.

Þorlákr's successor was his nephew – Páll Jónsson (1195–1211). Páll was an illegitimate son of "the greatest chieftain" – Jón Loptsson – and Þorlákr's sister – Ragnheiðr.[57] Páll studied abroad and by the 1190s had established himself as a chieftain at Skarð at Land. He had married young and was like his brothers Sæmundr and Ormr engaged in extending and consolidating their family's grip on Rangárþingi. According to the *Páls saga* during the elections at the Alþingi at 1194 it was decided that "Bishop Brandr should appoint the *electus* and he chose Páll Jónsson."[58] At first, Páll refused, following ecclesiastical tradition, but then accepted and rode together with his father and brothers to Skálholt.

Hólar bishopric

Due to his favour and will, the second bishopric of Iceland was founded during the lifetime of Gizurr. The first northern bishop was Jón Ögmundarson (1106–21). Jón was a foster son of Gizurr Ísleifsson and a third cousin of Teitr Ísleifsson's wife.[59] Fosterage was a complex institution. Taking on a boy meant alliance with his kin and when grown up he would be considered a son to his foster father and brother to his foster siblings. The foster child did not inherit from the fosterer but could in all other aspects be expected to behave toward a stepfather and his family like a son.[60]

Jón belonged to the family who promoted Christianity in their region. His father was Ögmundr Þorkelsson, the son of Ásgeir kneif, and his mother was Þorgerð Egillsdottir. Egill was a son of Hallr of Síða, "to whom it was granted to be first of all the chieftains in the East-fjord Quarter to accept baptism and the true faith"[61] and from whom at least six of the twelve Icelandic bishops in the Commonwealth period were descended. Þorgerð's mother was Þorlaugr, daughter of Þorvaldr from Ás. Jón's family estate was southern Breiðabólstaðr, a farm, and a church on Fljótshlíð. It was one of the richest and most important *staðir* in the country.[62] Vésteinsson[63] argues that St. Jón was a chieftain of his own family, whose absence from the area can hardly have been regretted by the neighbouring family of the Oddaverjar. It is not known into whose possession Breiðabólstadur came after Jón moved to Hólar, but shortly before 1200 it was held by one of the Oddaverjar.[64]

---

[57] see appendix 1B, 1C
[58] Páls saga, 2. Forward: Ps
[59] see appendix 1D
[60] Órri Vésteinsson 1996: 145
[61] Jsh, 1
[62] Órri Vésteinsson 1996: 147
[63] Ibid.
[64] Íslendingasaga, 38. Forward: Ís

Jón was married twice but childless, which probably could explain why he left his patrimony. On the other hand, he had strong connections with the North. Apart from northern relatives by marriage of Jón's foster father Gizurr – Hafliði Másson of Breiðabólstadur in Vesturhop and Ketill of Möddruvellir in Eyjafjörður, Jón's maternal line leads also to the North. Moreover, this line relates Jón to Gizurr's mother – Dalla. Dalla and Jón's maternal grandmother Þorlaug were sisters and daughters of Þorvaldr from Ás from the North. Geographically Ás is quite close to Hólar.

Jón moved to Hólar with his kinsmen. *Jóns saga helga* mentions at least two of them who gained a position in the cathedral's hierarchy – Jón's wife, who became a housekeeper of the cathedral estate and a priest called Hjalti, who became the second in authority over the cathedral estate after priest Hámundr Björnsson.[65]

The successor of Jón on the northern bishopric was Ketill Þorsteinsson (1122–45). He was a chieftain of the Mödruvellingar, one of the oldest and most respectable families in the north. Vésteinsson claims that Ketill was the last chieftain of his line and also the last chieftain who became a bishop.[66] Ketill was a son of Orstein, a son of Eyjólfr halti, a son of Guðmundr ríki, a son of Eyjólfr Valgerðarson. His cousins once removed were Björn, abbot of Þverá (1161–81) and Björn, bishop of Hólar (1147–62); his cousins in law were Þorlákr, bishop of Skálholt (1118–33) and future bishop of Hólar Brandr (1163–1201).[67] Bishop Ketill was also related by marriage to Bishop Gizurr: Gróa Gizurardóttir was Ketill's wife.[68]

A follower of Ketill in office, Björn Gilsson (1147–62), was of uncertain ancestry. His mother was a granddaughter of Þorfinnr karlsnefi in Staður in Reynines and her farther Björn or Þorbjörn seems to have been of considerable standing; his son Árni was a priest and his other daughter was married to the chieftain Þorsteinn ranglátr at Grund in Eyjafjörður.[69] It had been suggested that Björn had another son in Snorri, father of Grímr in Hof in Höfðaströnd; this would allow us to identify Bishop Björn's maternal family as minor chieftains in eastern Skagafjörður. Of Bishop Björn's paternal family we know that his sister, Þórný – mother of the chieftain Ormr Jónsson – was the daughter of Gils Einarsson. This link also places Björn's firmly among the most powerful families of Eyjafjörður.[70] His family may not have owned a chieftaincy but were, nevertheless, of high status. Björn is listed among the highborn priests of 1143.[71] Björn had been studying in Teitr Ísleifsson's school at Haukdælir and later he came for the same purpose to Hólar, to St. Jón's school. He may have

---

[65] Jsh, 14
[66] Órri Vésteinsson 1996: 149
[67] see appendix 1D
[68] see appendix 1A
[69] see appendix 1C
[70] Órri Vésteinsson 1996: 149–150
[71] DI, no. 186

remained at Hólar under Bishop Ketill and succeeded to the episcopacy with the support of his many powerful relatives and in-laws in the north and east.

Bishop Björn established a monastery at Þverá (1155–1551), on the lands of his ancestral estate. There is not much information about its activity, but the fact itself is significant.

Bishop Björn's successor became Brandr Sæmundarson (1163–1201).[72] Brandr's career up to his elections is unknown except that he was a priest and had been present at Bishop Björn's burial, which suggests that he had connections with the see before he became bishop. On his father's side, Brandr was from a side-branch of the Oddaverjar and Jón Loptsson accompanied him on his consecration journey to Norway in 1163/64, which suggests their influence on his appointment.[73] Bishop Brandr may have been a man with considerable local importance in Skagafjörður with close familial connections with some of the most powerful people in the quarter. Most probably, he inherited Staðr in Reynines and perhaps also his family chieftaincy. Therefore, he seems to be a protégé of the Oddaverjar. He had powerful relatives in the north and in the west as well as in Rangárþingi who doubtless considered him as their representative.

The table below presents the distribution of influence of the Icelandic powerful families over the bishoprics.

Skálholt:

Period:	Name:	Family:	Possession of a chieftaincy:
1056–1080	Ísleifr Gizurarson	Haukdælir	yes
1082–1118	Gizurr Ísleifsson	Haukdælir	yes
1118–1133	Þorlákr Runólfsson	Haukdælir	no
1134–1148	Magnús Einarsson	Haukdælir	no
1148	Hallr Teitsson	Haukdælir	yes
1152–1176	Klængr Þorsteinsson	Haukdælir	no
1178–1193	Þorlákr Þórhallsson	Oddaverjar	no
1195–1211	Páll Jónsson	Oddaverjar	yes

---

[72] see appendix 1C
[73] see appendix 1B

Hólar:

Period:	Name:	Family:	Possession of a chieftaincy:
1106–1121	Jón Ögmundson	Haukdælir	yes
1122–1145	Ketill Þorsteinsson	Húnröðlingar	yes
1147–1162	Björn Gilsson	Svínfellingar	yes
1163–1201	Brandr Sæmundson	Svínfellingar	yes

Most of the bishops of the period under consideration were a part of the Icelandic aristocratic network. Bishop Þorlákr Þórhallsson is the only exception. His family was neither influential nor respected, and he became a part of the network through his mother's and sister's connections.

At the top of this network were chieftains – the leaders of the most powerful families. Since there was no established Christian tradition on the island, bishops took up the political pattern of behaviour and influence of the secular leaders. Until the Gregorian reform movement started to make an impact on the Icelandic clergy, family with its wealth and power was the base of the bishops' authority. [74] Obviously, the bishops formulated policy in the interests of their families.

The Haukdælir family controlled the see at Skálholt from the founding of the office until the middle of the twelfth century. The two first bishops of Skálholt and founders of the office in Iceland – Ísleifr and Gizurr – were of chieftainly rank. They exercised authority on the basis of their secular status. After the death of Gizurr the bishop-chieftain pattern changed. Heads of the Haukdælir family lost interest in the office of the bishop. Absence of a heir could have been the reason – all Gizur's sons died before him. However, if we appeal to the customs of inheritance of chieftaincies, we will see that the chieftains rarely designated their successors. Primogeniture and legitimacy only occasionally make an appearance in the Commonwealth period.[75] A more like explanation lies in the fact that the office had not yet started to bring profit to its keeper since the tithe was only recently introduced and inefficiently collected. Nevertheless, the Haukdælir kept Skálholt under their control. The next two bishops – Þorlákr and Magnus – were distant relatives of Haukdælir, had respected ancestry, but not influential families. Bishop Þorlákr was adopted by Hallr Þórarinsson at Haukdælir; therefore as a foster son he was supposed to behave in the interests of the foster family. Remarkably, the Haukdælir had weight in the North – Bishop of Hólar, Jón Ögmundarson, was a foster son of Gizurr Ísleifsson

---

[74] The reform movement started by the Benedictine monastery at Cluny was supported by Pope Gregory VII. Normally the period of the Gregorian reform is limited to between 1046 (Council of Sutri) and 1085 (death of Gregory VII). The core of the movement was the fight for liberties of the Church (*libertas ecclesiae*). The reformers concentrated on simony, clerical marriage, and lay patronage. In the late 12th ct. the new issues arose, like codification of canon law, recent regulations on episcopal elections etc.

[75] Sigurðsson 1999: 95

and a distant relative of Haukdælir; Bishop Björn Gilsson was also adopted and educated by Hallr Þórarinsson. Family background defined the bishops' position in the aristocratic network. In view of the fact that Þorlákr and Magnús originated from less influential families, they tried to establish themselves in Icelandic aristocratic milieu by traditional means: through friendship with powerful men, gift-giving and delivering feasts.

The candidacy of Hallr Teitsson was an attempt by the Haukdælir to come back to the bishop-chieftain pattern. Hallr was a head of the family. This fact signifies the growing importance of the bishop's office in Skálholt diocese in the middle of the twelfth century. The office became profitable and chieftains wished to take it under the direct control.

The tenure of Bishop Klængr marked a shift of control over the see. Among his friends and relatives were heads of the dominant clans – the Haukdælir and the Oddaverjar. The successors of Klængr in office – bishops Þorlákr and Páll – were members of the Oddaverjar family. Apparently their candidatures to the see were a part of the alliance between the Haukdælir and the Oddaverjar who came to dominate the southern part of the country. The Haukdælir retained their influence over the see but allowed the Oddaverjar to select the bishops.[76] There is a significant difference between Þorlákr and Páll. Þorlákr's ancestry was neither respected nor influential. He was a new type of bishop, who tried to rely on a different source of authority – that of the Catholic Church. Owing to the fact that Þorlákr was the first elected candidate of the Oddaverjar at Skálholt and had none of the traditional sources of authority, we can suppose that the Oddaverjar, in promoting Þorlákr to office, wished to keep Skálholt bishopric in their full control. However, Þorlákr's policy deprived them of this possibility. The candidature of Bishop Páll was a return to the bishop-chieftain pattern.

The situation in the northern bishopric was different. All Hólar bishops, except Bishop Jón, were members of the local powerful families – the Svínfellingar and the Húnröðlingar – and chieftains by rank. However, none of them belonged to the dominant family of Skagafjörður – the Ásbirnings. All northern bishops were connected by family ties and/or education with the leaders of the South – the Haukdælir or the Oddaverjar – who obviously did not want to loose control over the North. The Oddaverjar drove the Haukdælir from the Northern bishopric in the middle of the twelfth century. Bishop Brandr came from the local powerful family, which was a side-branch of the Oddaverjar. Jón Loptsson accompanied him on his consecration journey to Norway in 1163/64. The tenure of powerful Bishop Brandr did not satisfy the Oddaverjar. The reason was a conflict between Sturla Þórðarson of Hvammur and Einarr Þorgilsson of Staðarhóll, where Brandr at first took the side of Sturla, his kinsman. However, Sturla's opponents, Guðmundr dýri and Jón Loptsson, were also Brandr's kinsmen; and towards the end of the feud Brandr joined their camp against Sturla. Brandr's position

---

[76] Órri Vésteinsson 1996: 159

derived from his family connections; therefore, the Oddaverjar could not entirely rely on him. The next protégé of the Oddaverjar became Þorlákr Þórhallsson, who had very weak position in the aristocratic network and was completely obliged to his patrons for his education and position. However, Bishop Þorlákr, lacking familial power as a basis for his own influence, started to rely on the authority of the Church and became an opponent of the Oddaverjar. The successor of Þorlákr, Bishop Páll, was a return to the bishop-chieftain pattern. Being an illegitimate son of the head of the Oddaverjar, Páll was well established in the aristocratic network of Iceland and protected the interests of his family.

The Ásbirnings managed to have their candidate elected to the Hólar see only in 1201, when the head of the family and the dominant chieftain of the North Quarter, Kolbeinn Tumason, promoted the priest Guðmundr Arason to the office. Guðmundr was a kinsman of Kolbeinn's wife; the two were first cousins on their father's side.[77] The second time a relative of the Ásbirnings became a bishop was in 1263. The priest Brandr Jónsson, a descendant of the Ásbirnings on his mother's side, was the bishop of Hólar in 1263–4.[78]

b) Election and consecration

In early medieval Europe canonical practice had evolved a system in which the critical and constitutive moments were the election and the consecration. Ecclesiastical office was thus, so to speak, elective and sacramental. Finally, by the 1160's the mature concept of *confirmatio* prescribed that the Episcopal jurisdiction of every bishop-elect derives from his consecration.[79] The common law provided several methods of Episcopal elections: *electio quasi per inspirationem, electio per compromissum* etc. The first one requires unanimity, which was naturally highly infrequent, the second one was in practice, but caused many difficulties. The electors of the candidacy were the members of a cathedral chapter; if one section of the chapter supported one candidate, and the other section, another candidate, and neither was willing to withdraw, Canon Law provided no simple solution. Eventually custom decided that the nominee of the majority should be regarded as elected. But the custom had no basis in actual legislation: the principal of numerical majority was not accepted in the medieval Church.[80]

The Icelandic pattern of selecting Icelandic bishops to the office until the second half of the twelfth century is not clear. Bishoprics did not have cathedral chapters to elect a bishop. Elections and announcement of a new bishop took place at the Alþing.

---

[77] Jón Jóhannesson 1974: 201
[78] Ibid., p. 259
[79] Benson 1968: 374
[80] Barraclough 1933: 276–7

According to *Hungrvaka* the first bishop – Ísleifr – was elected when it came to be necessary to choose a bishop. The men of the country had chosen Ísleifr who was "good looking, beloved of others, honest, generous".[81]

Ísleifr's son Gizurr was abroad when his father died and "the chieftains asked priest Guthorm to go abroad for the consecration."[82] However, when Gizurr came back and rode to the assembly the chieftains recognized him as the bishop-elect.

The election of the first northern bishop occured after the wish of Bishop Gizurr. According to both redactions of *Jóns saga helga*: "Northerners asked Bishop Gizurr to establish a bishopric in the northern Quarter, because... their Quarter was the most populous and the largest, and therefore had the greatest need of Episcopal visitation."[83] Such a wish – that the people asked a bishop to come/to rule them – was a part of the hagiographic tradition. The same had happened with the first two bishops – Ísleifr and Gizurr. Gizurr named the most distinguished candidate – Jón Ögmundarson.

There is a single instance in my material when the narrative mentions the appointment of a bishop by a chieftain. Hafliði Másson was so much affected by the conversation with Ketill that promoted him to the bishop's see at Hólar, which was vacant at that time. "This is my conviction: the people's interest will be best served if the choice is, as at present, that you become bishop."[84]

Gradually it became customary for bishops to approve a candidacy for the bishop-elect of the second see; importantly, he had to be a politically acceptable candidate to the chieftains. Sources mention elections, but alway with a single candidate. After elections a bishop-elect with a letter and a seal of an existing bishop went to the archbishopric for the consecration.

According to the sources, the first two bishops journeyed for their consecration not only to the archdiocesan see but also to Rome. Bishop Ísleifr was consecrated by Adalbert, the archbishop of Hamburg-Bremen, in 1056, upon direct instruction of a letter from Pope Leo IX (1049–54).[85] Only *Hungrvaka* recounts Ísleif's trip to the Holy See. *Saga Jóns biskups his elzta*, which builds its account of first two bishops largely on *Íslendingabók* by Ari the Wise, says that the consecration took place **in the days** of Pope Leo IX.[86] Peculiarly, Ari's account makes absolutely no mention either of German emperors or archbishops, or even German territories. This obvious omission might be a testimony to the political interests of Skálholt's ecclesiastics at the beginning of the twelfth century since

---

[81] Hungrvaka, 2
[82] Hungrvaka, 4
[83] Jsh, 7
[84] Þorgils saga ok Hafliða, 30. Forward: ÞsH
[85] Hungrvaka, 2; Jsh elzta, 1; Jsh Gunnlaug, 2. The latter, however, does not mention Pope Leo IX and adds that Ísleifr was consecrated by Adalbert at Herford. A translator of the Gunnlaug's text must have mixed up the information about Ísleif's consecration and a place of study.
[86] Jsh, 1

Íslendingabók is considered as an "official" history of the southern see. This issue needs further investigation.

Ísleif's trip to Rome indicates a good knowledge of who is who in medieval Europe in the second part of the eleventh century. At the time of Ísleifr, the papacy was still unreformed and the Church as a whole had no leader, only a nominal head. [87] Popes in the 1050s were closely related to the Emperors of the Holy Empire, who clearly controlled papal policy. The author of *Hungrvaka* recounts that before his trip to the Pope, Ísleifr visited the Emperor of the Holy Roman Empire – Henry III, to whom he presented a costly gift – a white bear from Greenland.[88] "A white bear gift" is a well-known literary motif, also appearing in *Auðunar þáttr vesfirska*, *Grænlendinga þáttr* from *Flateyjarbók* (ch. 6), *Vatndæla saga* (ch. 16), *Króka-Refs saga* (ch. 11, 12).[89] This motif likely derives from an older and more geographicly spread theme of "bear origin" that belongs to Scandinavian[90] mythological stock. For example, a bear's son tale appears in Danish and Icelandic narratives.[91] There is an allusion in *Hrolfs Saga Kraka* – a passage about Beorn and Bera and another one in *Saxo Grammaticus* – a story about the ancestors of Svein Estridson.[92] A common feature in both motifs is noble behaviour or "noble blood" of a character. In view of this clear and extensive literary motif, it seems safe to conclude that main intention of the author in recounting the dual trip and bear gift giving here was to demonstrate the high social standing of the first bishop to his audience.

On the ecclesiastical side, Ísleif's visit was not an obligatory one. According to Geoffrey Barraclough even the practice of metropolitans journeying to Rome for confirmation was only generally accepted at the end of the twelfth century and in the early thirteenth, and it took longer in outlying lands such as Lund. The first Archbishop of Lund to receive consecration at the hands of the Pope was Trigot who was elected in 1277. [93]

In 1082, Gizurr journeyed to Liemar, the archbishop of Bremen (1072–1101) for his consecration. During his trip, a quarrel arose between Emperor Henry IV and Pope Gregory VII, and the clergy were divided in their allegiance. Archbishop Liemar supported Henry IV. According to *Hungrvaka* and both redactions of *Jóns saga helga* Gizurr went to Rome for the consecration, which should signify for the audience that he supported Gregory VII. The Pope sent Gizurr to Archbishop Hartvig (1079–1102) of Magdeburg to be consecrated, who performed the Pope's command. There is no evidence to confirm that the fight for investiture had any important impact on the Icelandic Church.

---

[87] Brooke 1989: 24–5
[88] Hungrvaka, 2
[89] Hungrvaka, p. 7, ff. 4
[90] It can be also found in folklore of other nations; however, folklore data cannot be properly dated and need a particular approach
[91] Wright 1939: 126
[92] Saga of Hrolf Kraki, 18–20; Saxo Grammaticus, book 10, pp.407–8
[93] Barraclough 1934: 285–6

The situation with Gizur's Roman trips is analogous to his father's and might be an invention of the thirteenth century author. *Hungrvaka* was written in times of fierce political struggle between lay and ecclesiastic power in Norway. The leaders of Icelandic Church could not be pleased with constant interventions of the Norwegian archbishop in local church affairs. Contacts with Rome by the most prominent bishops of the country, Ísleifr and Gizurr, who were founders of the ecclesiastical office in Iceland, were the manifestation of their high status and demonstrated the highest authority for the Icelandic clergy. Roman trips of the first bishops were to demonstrate that these bishops were socially and politically important in their own right.

With the foundation of the archbishopric at Lund, Icelandic bishops went for their consecration to Denmark. Archbishop Özurr (Asser) (1102/3–37) consecrated four bishops-elect from Iceland: Jón Ögmundarson, Ketill Þorsteinsson, Þorlákr Runólfsson, and Magnús Einarsson.

Could an archbishop influence a bishop's candidacy? In the case with Bishop Jón we are told that the archbishop asked for the permission of the Pope, because Jón had two wives. The Pope sent Jón to Archbishop Özurr, "to whom he wrote under his seal giving him permission to consecrate St. Jón as bishop." However, it must be borne in mind that even in Europe Episcopal visitation was not in practice until the end of the twelfth century.

During the Hamburg-Bremen and Lund period of the Icelandic Church consecration of bishops had symbolic rather than political significance. Neither Hamburg-Bremen nor Lund archbishops had an interest in the Icelandic Church, and, thus, did not attempt to have influence over its leaders. The sources do not contain any objections from the Icelandic side to the subordination to the different archbishoprics.

Usually a bishop was selected after the death of his predecessor in office. Yet, there are two instances when an Icelandic bishop asked the archbishop to consecrate or to name his successor before his (the bishop's) death. Gizurr Ísleifsson made such a claim for the first time. Þorlákr Runólfsson was sent to the Archbishop of Lund to be consecrated. Since bishops in Iceland traditionally backed interests of their own/their patrons' family, it was desirable and profitable for the family to have its candidate elected. Bishop Klængr of Skálholt also selected his successor. The request of the Bishop, issued in 1173, is the first preserved documentary evidence of correspondence between Iceland and the Nidaros archbishopric.[94]

Jesse Byock says that absence of the competition in the Episcopal elections *de facto* is at variance with the situation on the continent and indicates political weakness of the office in Iceland.[95] He is not entirely right. First, the Church along with other institutions in Iceland were not stable, but in

---

[94]Regesta Norvegica, no. 147. Forward: Reg N
[95] Byock 1985: 8

the slow transformation. Rivalry about the position of bishops did not appear until the second part of the twelfth century because the ecclesiastical office was mainly controlled by one powerful family – the Haukdælir. Moreover, even in case of inheritance of politically far more important office, a chieftaincy, rivalry within one family does not appear to have been the norm.[96] The shift in the Episcopal elections in later period is discussed in more detail below. Second, it does not seem that public institutions of the island ever practised any kind of elections in European manner. A chieftaincy could be sold, given as a present, and inherited. In the last case all the legitimate sons were to decide among themselves who were to manage it. If a future leader was designated by his father, the choice was dictated by leader's personal qualities rather than legitimacy or primogeniture.[97] There are no data about the selection of a lawspeaker. However, the oldest and best source of information on the lawspeakers, Íslendingabók, does state where in the country they were from, so there is a reason to think that it was in part based on regional considerations.[98]

The Episcopal elections were becoming more and more crucial event towards the second part of the twelfth century. It was connected with the increase of influence of the other powerful families. On the death of Hallr Teitsson, the bishop-elect of Haukdælir family, Björn, the bishop of Hólar brought about the elevation of Hallr's successor. "It was the selection of everyone who was to decide, under the guidance of Björn, the bishop of Hólar" that Klængr Þorsteinsson should be *electus*.[99] Klængr was educated under St. Jón at Hólar, and later, as a cleric he has been living with the Bishop of Hólar Ketill.

At the Alþingi of 1174 three candidates were named: Abbot Þorlákr of Þykkvabær, Abbot Ögmundr Kálfsson, and the priest and chieftain in Reykholt Páll Sölvason.[100] Bishop Klængr was asked to decide on the candidate and he chose Þorlákr. The fact that the chieftain Páll Sölvason took part at the elections signifies that office of bishop restored its importance for chieftains. The figure of Þorlákr, who lacked traditional sources of power, also shows the wish of chieftains to get full control over the see.

Unlike the Hamburg-Bremen/Lund period, the consecration process in the Nidaros period became a means of Norwegian influence on Icelandic aristocratic families. The Nidaros archbishop actively interfered in Icelandic affairs. The Norwegian ecclesiastical party was keen on expanding its control over the bishoprics in the Orkney Islands, the Faeroe Islands, and the Isles of Man, which previously were under the jurisdiction of York, and by means of church organization to consolidate its

---

[96] Jón Viðar Sigurðsson 1999: 96
[97] Ibid., p. 94–5
[98] Gísli Sigurðsson 2004: 66–7
[99] Hungrvaka, 8
[100] Þs A, 9

power in Norway and abroad. The first letter of Archbishop Eystein, issued in 1173, was an attempt to establish control over the Icelanders not only in a religious but also in a secular sphere.[101] The letter concerns mainly ecclesiastical matters, but also regards relationships between Icelanders and Norwegian king: "also the Icelanders who offended against the king and his people must be fined."[102]

Bishop Klængr had to ask archbishop's permission to name his successor. The consecration of Bishop Þorlákr Þórhallsson is described in *Þorlákr's saga A*. On the bishop-elect's arrival in Norway, it appeared that King Magnús and his father Earl Erling opposed his consecration. The reason for the dispute is uncertain. The letter of Archbishop Eystein to the Icelanders tells that the reason for the rejection was a conflict between the Icelanders and the Norwegian king.[103] According to the saga Archbishop Eystein did not want to consecrate Þorlákr without the king's approval. Charles Joys argues that kings' unwillingness to approve Þorlákr was unexpected by Eystein.[104] Officially the Norwegian king had no direct influence on Iceland. The saga underlines the role and influence of Archbishop Eystein in the conflict. The description of the archbishop's courteous appeal for king's official permit for consecration of Þorlákr was aimed to show to the audience mutual respect between *regnum* and *sacerdotium*.

With the enthronement of King Sverre in Norway relationships between supreme secular and ecclesiastical powers became hostile and this influenced the consecration of Icelandic bishops. *Regesta Norvegica* (1153) contains a letter from bishops Tore of Hamar, Nikolas Arnesson of Olso, Njal of Stavanger, and Martin of Bergen. The bishops asked Archbishop Eirik to consecrate Páll Jónsson, bishop-elect of Skálholt.[105] The bishops obviously made such a request under the pressure of the king. Páll was a relative of King Sverre.[106]

On his arrival to Norway, Páll was kindly received by the king. Afterwards, he travelled to Denmark and was received by archbishops Eirik and Absalon most probably in a friendly manner. Absalon consecrated him after Eirik's wish, but he himself had no wish to do it. Páll came back to Norway and in some time sailed back to Iceland. To the point of view of Joys, consecration of Páll in Denmark happened due to the bishops' recommendations and according to King Sverre's will.[107] Why had the archbishop in exile consecrated an adherent of the opposite party, a chieftain, and a relative of the king? Probably, it was a consequence of some alliance contracted between Icelanders and the archbishop. Ecclesiastical leaders of Iceland tried to keep a balance in the conflict between *regnum* and *sacerdotium* and remain in good relationships with both sides. Sverre clearly had supporters in

---

[101] Reg N, no. 149
[102] Ibid. My translation.
[103] Órri Vésteinsson 1996: 154
[104] Joys 1948: 154–5
[105] Reg N, no. 228
[106] Páll's grandmother, Tora, was a daughter of Magnús Barefoot
[107] Joys 1948: 185

Iceland. The abbot of Þingeirar – Karl Jónsson – wrote the first part of the account about King Sverre. Pope Innocent III in his letter issued in 1198 found it necessary to warn Icelandic bishops against connections with the king.[108] On the other side, there is correspondence between the bishops and the Pope, Páll and Archbishop Eirik.[109] Bishops complain about supporters of Sverre and ask for the guidance and support of the Pope.[110]

Selection and consecration of the northern bishops was influenced firstly by the Haukdælir and later by the Oddaverjar families. The appointment of St. Jón, who was a foster son of Bishop Gizurr, to the see at Hólar, was an attempt by the Haukdælir to establish direct control over the North. Although succeeding bishops were members of the local powerful families – the Svínfellingar and the Húnröðlingar – they were linked with the Haukdælir and from the second half of the twelfth century with the Oddaverjar. The election of Bishop Ketill is a single instance of direct appointment to the Episcopal office by a chieftain.

---

[108] DI, no. 76
[109] Reg N, no. 246, 247, 248, 257, 297
[110] Reg N, no. 246

Chapter 2. Conflicts

In the following chapter I examine the bishops' role in conflicts.

Conflict is defined as a dispute about rights and interests between individuals and groups. It arises when the injured party reacts and tries to defend his threatened rights. The dispute may develop in many ways and the end is marked by a lasting settlement.[111] Study of bishops involvement into conflicts splits into two main parts: a) the partaking (in active or passive way)[112] in conflicts caused by others; and b) the causing of conflicts.

It is not necessary to differentiate between the types of conflicts proceeding from the object of a dispute. The thorough study of Jesse Byock explores this matter.[113] Nevertheless, there is a clear difference between the bishops' activities in feuds and in other kinds of conflict. The feud was the major part of Icelandic life and occupies a central position in Icelandic sagas.[114] A feud is a conflict between two groups, expressed as a sequence of one murder and a minimum of two following as revenge for the manslaughter. The participants of a feud are motivated by the necessity of vengeance and honour and are recruited on the basis of a duty to payback an encroachment of members of the group. The feud arises when a revenge murder was done, and ceases with a lasting desistance in a form of a compromise or a judgment.[115]

In feuds, the bishops either participated in peacemaking procedures, such as mediation and arbitrage, or joined one of the feuding parties. There are a number of conflicts, which fall out from the category of feud. Bishops' participation in such conflicts is limited to advice giving and supervision of the court's decision.

Which kind of conflicts did bishops take part in? Was there anything particular in their approach of reconciliation? How successful were bishops in peacemaking and advising; and how did it influence their position in society?

The second part of the chapter investigates conflicts caused by bishops. Major questions here are reasons, means, and success.

As was already pointed out above, the main partakers of feuds in Iceland were chieftains. Did feuding have the same significance for bishops as it had for chieftains? A comparison between chieftains' and bishops' ways of reconciliation and advice giving also takes place in the present study.

---

[111] Jón Viðar Sigurðsson 1999: 159–160
[112] Under the passive way of partaking I mean to be only a follower of the rival party without active participation.
[113] Byock 1982: 222–44
[114] Andersson and Miller 1989: 22
[115] Hansen 1999: 24

Moreover, working with the material I observed a considerable distinction in the politics of the bishops who owned a chieftaincy and the bishops without a chieftaincy. I examine these two patterns in connection with bishops' involvement into the conflicts.

a) Partaking in conflicts caused by others

Information about bishops' involvement in political issues is not equally provided by sources. The participation of bishops in feuds is mostly in the field of mediation and arbitrage. Nevertheless, there are a number of instances, which mention participation of the higher ecclesiastics, namely bishops Ísleifr Gizurarson, Gizurr Ísleifsson, and Magnús Einarsson not as neutrals, but as partisans. There is no information about the conflicts of bishops Jón Ögmundarson and Björn Gilsson.

The first two bishops – Ísleifr Gizurarson and Gizurr Ísleifsson – were from the Haukdælir family and owned a chieftaincy. In fact, we cannot call those instances the first two bishops took part in as conflicts in the meaning presented above. It was rather a number of disagreements between bishops and other persons. Hungrvaka states: "Ísleifr had great hardship in his bishopric because of deeds of disobedient men."[116] Further, we get more information about these cross-grained men. The author mentioned a lawspeaker who lived with both mother and her daughter and people who took part in Viking raids. In times of Ísleifr, morals were not considered to be in the competence of a bishop. Under a pressure of the Norwegian archbishop the end of the twelfth century this situation started to change.

Ísleif's son and the following bishop Gizurr deserved the most outstanding characteristics from the author of *Hungrvaka*. "...and thus, everybody freely followed his commands, young and old, rich and poor, women and men, and it is truly to say that he was both king and bishop over the land as long as he lived."[117] "It has been assumed among all the wise men that by the God's grace and of his own he was the most noble man in Iceland among both clerics and laity."[118] There are different interpretations of Gizur's image in *Hungrvaka*. From the viewpoint of Nordal, the abovementioned statement from *Hungrvaka* seems to be entirely correct. The great landowners of the Saga Age had passed out of the picture; the chieftains of the Sturlung Age had not yet arrived on the scene.[119] Jóhannesson explains such a characteristic of Gizurr's episcopacy also by favourable natural

---

[116] Hungrvaka, 2.
[117] Hungrvaka, 4. It should be mentioned that the theme "a king of Iceland" for the first time appers in *Hungrvaka* and is combined with the top of the Church organization of the country. In its further development the looses assosiations with bishops. See more in: Andersson, Th. M. 1999, "The king of Iceland." Speculum, 74 (4), 923–34
[118] Hungrvaka, 5
[119] Sigurður Nordal 1990: 239, 241

conditions and general prosperity at this period.[120] The success of Gizurr's rule was measured by the ancient belief of a link between country's prosperity and a ruler and numerous disasters that occurred immediately after his death.[121] Traditionally the period from the end of the Saga Age to the death of Bishop Gizurr (1030–1118) has been called the "Age of Peace" (*friðaröld*). This concept, as it was observed by Byock, was by no means invented by adhearents of book-prose theory and has its roots in the thirteenth century source – *Kristini saga*, which most likely reflect the bias of clergy.[122]

The author of *Hungrvaka* living at the peak of papal might most likely made a use a pattern of the Christian leader circulated in the secular and ecclesiastical milieu of Europe. Besides, Gizurr was only one bishop-chieftain among all mentioned in *Hungrvaka*. Hiis father, Ísleifr, it not considerd, because during his office authority of the bishop at Skálholt was still doubtful. The rest of the bishops of Skálholt were of respected ancestry, but did not own a chieftaincy. *Hungrvaka* was composed on the period, when the Icelanders came back to the bishop-chieftain pattern. Political pattern of chieftains was a model for bishops. Gizurr was primarily a prominent chieftain; this might be one of the reasons why the author depicted Gizurr as an ideal bishop.

Bishop Magnús falls into the second category of bishops, those without a chieftaincy. His family background was similar to his predecessor in office. Bishop Magnús was Bishop Þorlákr's first cousin once removed and a distant relative of Haukdælir. In the eyes and pen of the author of *Hungrvaka* he was doing well in settling disputes. "It turned out soon how exellent he was in his generosity and management of his own and other's matters, …and therefore, no conflicts occurred between men while Magnús was a bishop."[123] Even his entry to the General Assembly after the consecration brought a settlement to a disagreement. From the passage in *Hungrvaka* is clear that Magnús participated in mediation and/or world arbitration. Unfortunately, it is the only available information about the bishop; there is no other account about him in my material.

Vésteinsson claims that for the author of *Hungrvaka* Magnús is probably the ideal bishop, because he was not only committed to peace, but also had the means to make it.[124] The author, to the point of view of Vésteinsson, was an adherent of the existing order but not of supremacy of the Church.[125]

In my opinion, information about Magnús is too scarce to say something definite about his peacemaking activity. The most outstanding characteristic is given by author of *Hungrvaka* to Gizurr Ísleifsson. However, if we compare some Gizur's characteristics with the image of Magnús, an analogous picture will appear. Both bishops were praised for their reconciliation activities and peace

---

[120] Jón Jóhannesson 1974: 148
[121] Ibid.
[122] Byock 1985: 4, 6
[123] Hungrvaka, 8
[124] Órri Vésteinsson 1996: 162
[125] Ibid.

during their tenure. The authority of Gizurr in *Hungrvaka* is described as the unconditional one – "everybody freely followed his commands" – but in the case of Magnús, this quality vanishes. Instead, the author concentrated on the means of reconciliation. These were: wealth and its proper use in the form of gift giving and feasts, and personal skills. Magnús "never spared his property during his tenure to reconcile those who disagree with each other."[126] Gift exchange and holding of feasts were the means to strengthen ones position in society. There are a number of studies dealing with gifts and gift exchange in pre-modern societies.[127] In Scandinavian material, the theme of feasts and gift exchange has been examined by Jón Viðar Sigurðsson.[128] He underlines the importance of holding feasts and gift giving for the authority and prestige of chieftains. Anthropologist Ross Samson points out unequal relations of power, which are reflected in the nature of exchange. The giving of gifts, if reciprocated roughly equally over a long period, is balanced.[129] Lavish feasts were a method of securing loyalty of the guests and, consequently, social position of the powerful chieftains.[130] That is why it was so important to keep holding feasts and gift-exchanges over a long period of time. Bishop Magnús made use of traditional means to get influence – gifts and feasts – that were also used by the chieftains to the same purpose.

A sufficient number of studies examine ways of reconciliation in Icelandic society. Byock distinguishes three major categories in the process of resolution: a) arbitrated settlement, whether in or out of court; b) direct settlement between the concerned parties, whether violent or peaceful; and c) the rejection of an offer of resolution.[131]

Sigurðsson underlines that fewer than 10% of conflicts in the Commonwealth period were dealt with by courts; more than nine out of ten conflicts were resolved through arbitration or direct negotiation.[132] He also shows the elements that formed the process of resolution: mediation, arbitration/self-judgment, and use of the courts and agreement.[133]

In my material bishops take part only in mediation and arbitrage. Although, according to *Grágás* bishops could judge priests in ecclesiastical matters; I have not found a single instance of such procedures.[134]

The aim of mediators in *Sturlunga saga* is to achieve the assent of the opponents for arbitration (*gerð*) and to keep the peace until the decision was made known. Mediators also guarantee a temporal

---

[126] Hungrvaka, 8
[127] Vestergaard 1991; Mauss 1969; Gurevich 1984
[128] Jón Viðar Sigurðsson 1999: 90–2
[129] Samson 1991: 90
[130] Sigurður Nordal 1998: 156
[131] Byock 1982: 259
[132] Jón Viðar Sigurðsson 1999: 182–3
[133] Ibid, p. 160
[134] Grágás I, K 5. Forward: Grg I

truce (*grið*) until the parties could hold a meeting.[135] Mediators were not involved in the case directly, but, nevertheless, participated in it. Mediators could give the parties their views on the situation and their advice, including saying what they believed to be the best interests of the parties. In this way they could help them to reach a decision.[136] An arbiter is a person empowered to make a decision and whose candidacy is agreed on by both sides. There are two representative examples of mediation and arbitrage: a feud between Þorgils Oddason and Hafliði Másson in the beginning of the twelfth century and a conflict between Sturla Þorðarson and Einar Þorgilsson in the second half of the century. I will examine these two in details.

Bishop Þorlákr Runólfsson was a mediator in a feud between Þorgils Oddason and Hafliði Másson in 1117–21. As bishop of Hólar, Ketill Þorsteinsson was also a mediator of the dispute, but his way of reconciliation was absolutely different. Mediation of this feud requires separate examination. Bishop Þorlákr was of respected ancestry but under the control of the Haukdælir family. The change of pattern from a bishop-chieftain to a bishop who did not own a chieftaincy most likely happened because of coincidence. The sons and heirs of Bishop Gizurr, who might be interested in the office of bishop, died before him. Subsequent bishops had to search for resources to strengthen their authority. Iceland did not inherit any Christian tradition to stand by as it was in Europe. Icelandic bishops concentrated on the legislative and mediating activity, which was highly valued in the country.Chieftain Hafliði Másson was one of the most respected and powerful chieftains in Iceland of his time. Chieftain Þorgils Oddason acquired his chieftaincy just before the conflict arose. The conflict lasted from 1117 to 1121 and had several stages; each of them finished with some kind of resolution, but did not bring the feud to the end. The matter grew more and more serious and at the General Assembly in 1120 is reached the phase of the open confrontation. Þorgils was declared an outlaw and did not let Hafliði confiscate his property. The fight between these two was prevented by the third group of men under the leadership of the chieftains Þórðr Gilsson of Fell at Fellsströnd and Húnbogi Þorgilsson from Skarð at Skarðströnd and other powerful men. The culmination of the conflict occurred at the General Assembly in 1121. Both parties gathered armed forces and Þorgils, an outlaw, was going to ride to the Assembly.

There were several attempts at mediation of the conflict: in 1118, 1120, and in 1121. The last stage assembled a number of powerful men, and among them the Bishop of Skálholt, Þorlákr, and a future bishop of Hólar, priest Ketill Þorsteinsson.

---

[135] Kulturhistorisk leksikon for nordisk middelalder fra vikingetid til reformationstid V: gerð, grið. Forward: KLNM
[136] Jón Viðar Sigurðsson 1999: 161

A future bishop-elect of Skálholt Hallr Teitsson took part in the conflict on the side of Hafliði. Hallr was Hafliði's cousin in law; his sister was a second wife of Hafliði. Hallr actively participated in the lawsuit, but will not be considered here.[137]

Bishop Þorlákr and priest Ketill were related to Hallr and, therefore, through Hallr to Hafliði Másson. Þorlákr was a descendant of Ketilbjön gamli like the Haukdælir and from Ögmundr bíldr like St. Jón.[138] He was also the great-nephew of Hallr Þórarinsson, who adopted and educated him in Haukdælir.[139] Together with Þorlákr, Hallr Þórarinsson adopted Teitr Ísleifsson, whose son Hallr participated in the conflict. Besides, Þorlákr was promoted to the office by Bishop Gizurr Isleifson, a brother of Teitr.

Þorlákr did not possess a chieftaincy and his position in the Haukdælir family was certainly subordinate. He was also related to Þorsteinn ranglátr, who appears to have supported Þorgils Oddason.

Priest and chieftain Ketill Þorsteinsson was related to Haukdælir by marriage. His wife was Gróa, a daughter of Bishop Gizurr. Bishop Þorlákr was his cousin in law.

Altogether, the saga names ten mediators who took part in the reconciliation of this conflict. Four of the ten mediators experienced divided of loyalties because of their kinship and personal relationships with both Þorgils and Hafliði.[140] Both Ketill and Þorlákr fall into this category as relatives of Hafliði's wife. Yet, the results of their attempts were dissimilar. Þorlákr absolutely failed in his mediation, but Ketill became a key person, who managed to persuade Hafliði to start the process of reconciliation. This mediation also became a landmark in Ketill's career. Hafliði was so much effected by the conversation with Ketill that he promoted him to the bishopric at Hólar, which was vacant at that time. "This is my conviction: the people's interest will be best served if the choice is, as at present, that you become bishop."[141]

Why was Þorlákr's mediation ineffective? Remarkably, the author focused on two conversations between Hafliði and bishops. There were other mediators in the conflict, each of them attempting to convince opponents, but the author is not interested in recording their speeches. Maybe, their arguments are known to the audience too well and there was no reason to write them down. The author records unusual arguments instead and shows one of them ended in failure and the other one

---

[137] Hallr's attitude to the conflict is depicted as a quite bizarre one. On request of his cousin in law he gives him support, but says to one man: "The only man who is my friend is the man who will not support this suite." (Ch. 21) In the next chapter, he "urged Hafliði and his men to ride against Þorgils with the forces they had collected together, declaring that it was utterly disgraceful and outside the law for outlawed men to ride to a hallowed Þing." At the end of the dispute, he became the one who was "in every way harder to persuade than Hafliði". (Ch. 31).
[138] Órri Vésteinsson 1996: 147
[139] Hungrvaka, 6
[140] Jón Viðar Sigurðsson 1999: 162
[141] ÞsH, 30

with success. Bishop Þorlákr in his mediation refers to the authority of the Church and promises Hafliði a reward in the afterlife. Apparently, it was not a sound argument for Hafliði. In his second try, he orders Hafliði to stop the feud: "and by the power which God gave to the Apostle Peter to bind and to loose the whole of heaven and earth, and which he then gave to Pope Clement[142], following whom one after the other took up that power, which Archbishop Özurr passed on me – now with that power and authority I do here forbid you to remain here, to refuse reconciliation, and so destroy the peace."[143]

Þorlákr did not rely on the authority of the kin, he was depended from the Haukdælir, and, therefore, his own family was not an influential one. A family determined the bishop's place in the Icelandic aristocratic network. Þorlákr's position was weaker in comparison with Ketill's. Ketill possessed a chieftaincy and was married to a daughter of the powerful bishop-chieftain Gizurr. The authority of the Apostle Peter and the fourth Roman Pope Clement was meaningless in the milieu of Icelandic chieftains. A passage from *Þorláks saga B* gives an example of similar opposition. The authority of Apostles, Holy Fathers of the Church, popes, Canon Law, and the archbishop are opposed to the authority of forebears, laws of the land and customary usage.[144]

Overall, Þorlákr's episcopate saw a series of conflicts. This is reflected in *Hungrvaka*: "Many chieftains were difficult to Bishop Þorlákr because of their disobedience, but some because of their evil life and lawbreaking..."[145]

Bishop Þorlákr also initiated the writing of the Christian Law section. There is an obvious link between failures of the Bishop in mediation/reconciliation of the feud and writing down of laws. The possession of a book itself signalled authority and power of its owner.[146] On the other hand, legislative activity signalled the power of the bishop and was meaningful for the chieftains who used the same means to draw a line between them and society.[147]

Priest Ketill accomplished his task. Ketill's way to bring Hafliði to reconciliation was to tell his own example. This example bears features of Christian doctrine: humility and a search for God's advice. At this point, I agree with Miller that Christianity gave peacemakers a new stock of arguments urging forbearance and forgiveness.[148] On the other hand, the whole speech is delivered in the frames of Icelandic legal tradition, which concentrates on keeping order more than justice. Ketill behaved

---

[142] According to Tertullian, writing c. 199, the Roman Church claimed that Clement was ordained by St. Peter (De Praescript., xxxii), and St. Jerome tells us that in his time "most of the Latins" held that Clement was the immediate successor of the Apostle (De viris illustr., xv). St. Jerome himself in several other places follows this opinion, but here he correctly states that Clement was the fourth pope.
Source: www.newadvent.org
[143] ÞsH, 28
[144] Þorláks saga B, 21. Forward: Þs B
[145] Hungrvaka, 7
[146] Mc Guire 1999: 108
[147] Jón Viðar Sigurðsson 1999: 177
[148] Miller 1990: 268

wisely and, as a result, received honour and benefits from his personal abuse. Talking about Ketill's reconciliation we should also bear in mind his position and family ties in the aristocratic milieu. Ketill was a well-connected chieftain and Hafliði did not lose honor accepting his advice.

The figure of Hallr Teitsson, who unluckily died before being consecrated, was an interesting try of the Haukdælir family to come back to the bishop-chieftain pattern. The bishop of Skálholt was becoming a more powerful and influential figure. The office promised economical advantages to its keeper, since the bishop's part of tithe was collected at Skálholt. Perhaps, the feud between Þorgils and Hafliði and the leading role of bishops in its reconciliation has played a decisive role in the change of the pattern. Bishops intervened into the legislative process, which previously had been exclusively in competence of chieftains.

Information about bishops' activities in political matters is not equally provided by sources. A more balanced picture starts with bishops Klængr of Skálholt and Brandr of Hólar. Both Klængr and Brandr were involved in the feud between Sturla Þórðarson of Hvammur and Einarr Þorgilsson of Staðarhóll. The conflict lasted for about fourteen years and was the object of several attempts of reconciliation. The confrontation started when it became known that the chieftain Þorvarð Þorgeirsson, Sturla Þórðarson's in-law, fathered a child by Yngvild Þorgilsdóttir. Einarr, Yngvild's brother, demanded inquiries and, at the end, ordeal. Bishop Klængr was to arbitrate. Þorvarð was cleared of the charge and Einarr was to pay a fine.[149] Later, it became known that the ordeal was faked and Sturla had a hand in the deception. Einarr turned his enmity against Sturla. Einarr's fine remained unpaid. The matter was raised at the General Assembly. Both Einarr and Sturla were sentenced to lesser outlawry. The following summer Einarr burned and robbed Sturla's farm – Hvammur. Bishop Klængr was asked to arbitrate. His decision did not satisfy Sturla and the conflict went on. It culminated in an open confrontation between the troops of Sturla and Einarr in 1171, which Sturla won. The mediation of friends convinced opponents to accept arbitration of the two most powerful chieftains Jón Loptsson and Gizurr Hallsson. The confrontation came to an end.[150]

Vésteinsson argues that this type of conciliation was very different: the Bishop took sides and supported some chieftains against others.[151] To my mind, the bishop to a certain extent played with each side and it was a consequence of his family background – he was related to the both rival powerful families. *Hungrvaka* claims that "Klængr was so such helper in the lawsuits, when he was asked for assistance. He was a great chieftain because of both wisdom and rhetoric. He had knowledge

---
[149] Hvamm-Sturla saga, 9. Forward: HSs
[150] HSs, 22
[151] Órri Vésteinsson 1996: 162

of laws of the country."[152] The bishop was educated at Hólar School and was promoted to the office by his relative and the Northern Bishop Björn. He did not own a chieftaincy, however, he was well connected. Among his friends and relatives were the most powerful chieftains – Jón Loptsson, Gizurr Hallsson, Þorgils Oddason, and Guðmundr Arason. As a bishop, he was an acceptable figure for both prominent families the Haukdælir and the Oddaverjar. Yet, Klængr was an imprudent politician. The ordeal of Þorvarð Þorgeirsson was solved in favour of the accused and, consequently, his relative and protector, Sturla Þórðarson. Einarr, an accuser, was to pay a fine. On the next stage of the feud, Bishop Klængr was chosen as an arbiter. However, this time his verdict was absolutely unprofitable for Sturla, but lucrative for Einarr. Most essentially, the peace was not achieved. The most important thing for Icelandic society was to bring parties to reconciliation and to stop a conflict.[153]

A final settlement was reached ten years later with the arbitration of the most influential chieftains – Gizurr Hallsson and Jón Loptsson. Bishop Brandr joined the conflict after the failed attempt of arbitration by Bishop Klængr. Family ties defined his choice and Brandr directly took the side of Sturla, his kinsman. However, Sturla's opponents – Guðmundr dýri and Jón Loptsson – were also Brandr's kinsmen; and in the 1180s Brandr joined their camp against Sturla.

It seems that the unsteady position of Klængr did not please the chieftains. The next bishop of Skálholt became a person closely connected with his patron – Þorlákr Þórhallsson. Besides, the economy of the see under Klængr, who spent wealth to gain more supporters, was ruined. The candidacy of Þorlákr Þórhallsson who was known as a good economist was supposed to recover the financial situation.

The tenure of Bishop Brandr was remarkable for its recurrence to the pattern of bishop-chieftain in the light of Gregorian reform movement, which eventually reached Iceland. In 1163, bishop-elect Brandr, accompanied by chieftain Jón Loptsson attended a synod at Bergen, where he was consecrated. In the synod, Archbishop Eystein Erlendsson brought about the election in of King Magnus Erlingsson and received from the king a proclamation of privileges for the Norwegian Church. During the coronation of King Magnus the legal basis of the royal succession was established – *Tronfølgeloven*. The ecclesiastics got the right to distinguish between legitimate and illegitimate sons of the king and to pose the right of primogeniture. If an heir was considered to be inadequate, a commission consisted of bishops, abbots, the *hirð*, and twelve of the wisest persons from each bishopric, who should name a proper heir from royal line.[154] This law has never been exercised. Reforms gave ecclesiastics a new status and authority, recognized by the secular power. However, Brandr did not invent any of them in Iceland. He was the man of considerable local importance in

---

[152] Hungrvaka, 9
[153] Jón Viðar Sigurðsson 1994: 131, 183
[154] Latinske documenter til norsk historie, no. 111. Forward: Lat Doc

Skagafjörður with close familial connections with some of the most powerful men in the quarter. Besides, he descendant from a side-branch of Oddaverjar, who must have promoted him to the office. He might have inherited Staður in Reynines and his family's chieftaincy, although it is not known whether the Reynistaðarmenn owned a chieftaincy.[155] Brandr's son Þorgeirr was married to Guðný, a daughter of the chieftain and courtier of King Inge – Þorvárð Þorgeirson from Eyjafjörðr.[156] Hvamm-Sturla and Guðmundr dýri were Brandr's third cousins. In the conflict of Hvamm-Sturla and Einarr he maintained Sturla's side; however, some years later all his support was given to Guðmundr dýri.

Brandr was an active participant of the political game in Iceland, and his means were of a traditional form. Bishop's political preferences were determined by blood relations and friendship. He successfully acted as a mediator and an arbiter in the major conflicts.[157] Unlike his predecessors, the author of the saga also mentions him giving advice: twice to the farmers, twice to the highborn men.[158]

Despite the fact that the bishop was not a fighter for *libertas ecclesiae*, he, nevertheless, to some extent followed the Gregorian movement. There are two instances: one of church property and one of legitimacy of marriage.[159] I examine these issues in the second part of the chapter. Brandr also had close contacts with Archbishop Eystein; a son of the Bishop, Þorgeir, who stayed one winter with the archbishop.[160]

The appointment of Bishop Páll Jónsson was clearly a reaction to the troublesome episcopate of Bishop Þorlákr Þórhallsson. Páll was a chieftain and fully supported his brother and the head of the Oddaverjar family, Sæmundr. The main long-lasting conflict in the times of Bishop Páll was caused by his colleague from the northern bishopric, Bishop Guðmundr Arason. The author of *Páls saga* informs us that Páll was put in an awkward position, because "the archbishop had sent him letters under his seal, telling him to support and assist the cause of Bishop Guðmundr as well as he could, but many of Bishop Páll's dearest friends, his relatives and in-laws supported Kolbeinn."[161] Páll tried to mediate in the conflict and offered his support to Guðmundr if he gave up his demands.[162] Guðmundr rejected, and in the future Páll did not oppose the chieftains chasing him. Páll's participation in feuds was similar to that of Bishop Brandr. Both of them were a part of the secular network and referred to the most powerful chieftains as to the supreme authority in complicated cases; both took part in major conflicts as arbitrators, mediators, and also consultants.

---

[155] Órri Vésteinsson 1996: 152
[156] Guðmundar saga biskups, 6. Forward: Gsb. According to the saga 600 guests were present on the wedding celebration, which also shows Brandr's wealth.
[157] Guðmundar saga dýra, 9, 15, 18. Forward: Gsd
[158] Gsd, 4, 16, 20
[159] Gsd, 11. Bishop proclaimed himself an heir of a cleric; Gsd, 9. Children of Ingebjörg and Þorfinn were announced to be born out legal wedlock.
[160] Gsb, 11
[161] Ps, 15
[162] Ibid

All in all, I count five instances of arbitration in my sources; two of them were arbitration of ordeals, where bishops were sole arbitrators; two times more bishops arbitrated solely; in one case a chieftain and two bishops arbitrated jointly.[163] It should be noted that the ordeal was not central to the Icelandic system of proof.[164] Ordeal is prescribed only in parentage cases where as a means of proof it could replace or outweigh a panel verdict.[165]

Mediation of bishops appears in five cases. Almost all of them were the chief feuds of the time. The bishop could mediate alone, lead a group of clergy, or join a chieftain. There are a number of cases, where the authors of the sagas underline peace during the tenure and ascribe it to the activity of a bishop – three instances. Byock claims that mediation of the bishops was an exclusive feature of the Icelandic state system.[166] However, the portrayal of pacifying clerics seems to be commonplace in Christian writings. The bishop's role as a peacemaker was an essential element of his function in the Christian church from the first centuries of its establishment.[167]

In five instances bishops joined a certain side in open confrontations: in three cases bishops backed their patrons; two others concerned Bishop Brandr who played an active and decisive role in the conflicts.[168]

In one case, the bishop was supervising the court's decision. In the lawsuit between Þórðr Ívarsson against Jón Húnröðarson Bishop Brandr and his son Þorgeir backed Þórðr. Jón was declared an outlaw. The Bishop, his son, their relatives and friends all together journeyed to assist at the court of execution of Jón's outlawry.[169] Interestingly, the outcome of the affaire with Jón's outlawry finished with "that the dispute was placed under the bishop's jurisdiction."[170]

There are eight examples of bishops giving advice: three of them – to highborn men, four – two of the low status, and one – to a highborn priest.[171]

This last one is a single instance of Bishop Þorlákr as an advice giver. There are no means to verify reliability of the occasion. The situation itself is doubtful. Priest Þórir entrusted the administration of his property to his kinsman Páll Sölvason the priest while he and his wife were abroad. Þórir, his wife and their son died on the way and Páll inherited Þórir's possessions. A member of the Sturlung family Böðvar Þórðarson proclaimed Þórir's sister Vigdís a rightful heir and started to

---

[163] Gsd, 9; HSs, 9; Gsb, 9; HSs, 10; Gsd, 15
[164] Andersson and Miller 1989: 36
[165] Grágás II, no. 49, 71, 233. Forward: Grg II
[166] Byock 1988: 154–5
[167] www.newadvent.org
[168] HSs, 19. The involvement of bishops Klængr and Brandr in the conflict between Einarr and Sturla is counted in two cases; Ps, 15. I consider archbishop's warning and order to support Bishop Guðmundr in his confrontation with the chieftains as indirect evidence of Bishop Páll's participation in clashes; Gsd, 18; Gsb, 15
[169] Gsb, 9
[170] Ibid.
[171] Ps, 10; Ís, 20; Gsd, 4; Gsd, 16; Gsd , 4; Gsd , 7; Gsd , 20; HSs, 34

fight for her interests. The conflict was getting serious and gradually involved the most powerful men of the country. The situation was worsened by Páll's wife; during negotiations she injured a supporter of Böðvar, the chieftain Sturla Þórðarson. Páll realized that he could not oppose Sturla alone and searched for the support of other powerful men. At this moment he "went to meet Bishop Þorlákr and talked to him."[172]

Actually, at the moment Páll Sölvason went to the bishop, he had already got the support of chieftains Jón Loptsson, Guðmundr dýri, and Bishop Brandr. Why did he search for the advice of much less influential Þorlákr? We might suggest that it was connected with Þorlákr's campaign for Church's authority over ecclesiastical property. But Þórir's belongings went to Páll on the basis of their kinship, not an order. Bishop Þorlákr's advice "to carry a weapon in order to defend yourself if you have need to do so" contravenes Þorlákr's policy.[173] Although there is no independent evidence that he campaigned against clerics bearing arms, the ban for clerics to carry weapons was among requests of Archbishop.[174] It is unlikely that Þorlákr would confront the archbishop's policy. Proceeding from what was said above I would doubt Þorlákr's participation in the conflict. It seems as if the author of the saga, knowing the bishop's policy, added him into the number of prominent characters of the appropriate case. The author connects Þorlákr to the plot some chapters earlier – no one else except the bishop hears the news about the death of Þórir and brings them to Iceland.[175]

What was the difference of the bishops' peacemaking and the one of the chieftains? Sigurðsson claims that the chieftains rarely took part in the mediation of disputes; however, they sat in almost 75% of arbitration juries because, as the most powerful people in society, they were the only ones who could settle conflicts.[176]

The study above has showed that partaking of bishops was equal in arbitration and mediation, and altogether their contribution in the peacemaking concerned only significant cases, the feuds of the most powerful chieftains.

The method of arbitration by chieftains can be studied on the case of a priest and the chieftain Páll Sölvason from Reykjaholt. I shall compare this case with the one where an arbiter was a bishop. The contents of Páll's case have been narrated above. Here I shall concentrate on its reconciliation. The first attempt of reconciliation by a judge, Jón Loptsson, was rejected by Páll's opponent.[177] In some time, parties assembled forces and went to the Alþingi to find a solution. Mediators tried to bring opponents to the second attempt; their main arguments were: a) the necessity to stop the conflict; b)

---

[172] HSs, 34
[173] Ibid.
[174] Órri Vésteinsson 1996: 170; Lat Doc, no. 163
[175] HSs, 30
[176] Jón Viðar Sigurðsson 1999: 184
[177] HSs, 30

the break of the first agreement and dishonour; and c) the prestige of accepting the new arbitration of Jón Loptsson.[178] Both sides acknowledged a new resolution. The settlement was affirmed with banquets and gift giving, and bound by fosterage – Sturla's son Snorri was fostered by Jón Loptsson.[179] The emphasis of the mediators was laid on the position of the judge and the honour of the adversaries.

An example of a bishop's judgement can be found in the feud between the chieftains Hvamm-Sturla and Einarr Þorgilsson. The verdict of Bishop Klængr did not satisfy Sturla, because it was unfair and Sturla lost his honour. In many ways arbitration was a face-saving procedure. It relied upon the understanding that the honour of all parties had to be considered.[180] The feud between Einarr and Sturla continued until mediators managed to convince rivals to accept the verdict of the third party. The heads of two most influential families become arbitrators – the Haukdælir and the Oddaverjar – Gizurr Hallsson and Jón Loptsson respectively. Here loss of honour caused the failure of reconciliation; respect for the judges kept the solution.

All in all, there is only one instance of a successful bishops' verdict. It was the joint arbitration of Bishops Páll and Brandr and the chieftain Jón Loptsson.[181] In other cases we are not told about the outcome of the affair.

There is one instance of successful mediation. It was Bishop Ketill's mediation in the conflict between Þorgils Oddasson and Hafliði Másson. Ketill's method of reconciliation was based on retelling his own story and Christian virtues. Miller claims that Christianity provided the first steps towards the institutionalisation of peacemaking and the arbitration processes, even when their structural position relative to the disputants was not such as to make them natural interveners responsibility. To his point of view priests and bishops also figured actively in the peacemaking and arbitration processes, even when their structural position relative to the disputants was not such as to have made them natural interveners had they not been in holy orders.[182]

In my material I have not found cases where bishops were participating in mediation/arbitrage without been related to the main participants. Indeed, in theory, Christianity obliged men of holy orders to bring reconciliation among the rival parties. However, as Miller notices their "profession did not always prevent priests from behaving like other feuding partisans."[183] There are instances where bishops joined one of the rival parties.[184] In practice, bishops advanced the interests of their families.

---

[178] HSs, 34
[179] HSs, 35
[180] Byock 1982: 103–4
[181] Gsd, 15
[182] Miller 1990: 268
[183] Ibid.
[184] HSs, 19; Ps, 15

Family links determined the bishops' position in the aristocratic network and largely defined the bishop's capability to participate in and influence conflicts. Distant relatives of the powerful families and bishops without a chieftaincy could not influence the political game in Iceland due to their position in the aristocratic milieu. As for Ketill's mediation, I should underline his position in the network and the intelligent way the mediation was held. Wisdom, knowledge of law, and patience were characteristics of a successful chieftain.[185] Indeed, successful chieftains were the role-models for the bishops.[186]

Religious and secular power in Iceland was closely connected. In Ari's register of the most powerful priests from about 1143, forty priests are mentioned,[187] thirteen of whom were chieftains. During that period there were about twenty-seven chieftains in the country as a whole.[188] The important part played by the chieftains in conflicts and their resolution meant that virtually all lawsuits were simultaneously political disputes.[189] Proceeding from the fact that bishops took part in the major conflicts of the country we can conclude that they were also players of the political game. However, considering the length of the period and frequency of disputes, the percentage of bishops' participating in disputes was exceedingly small. Indeed, in the field of peacemaking the Christian model of bishop and the Icelandic model of chieftain overlapped; bishops were supposed to bring reconciliation and keep peace. Nevertheless, in Icelandic politics only bishops of chieftainly rank were successful in mediation and arbitrage.

Until the Gregorian movement started to make an impact on Icelandic clergy and until the appearance of clergy who relied on the authority of the Church, bishops had no means to increase their power except by traditional methods: which is the authority of the family, feasts, gifts, personal skills, and alliances with mighty men. Successful intervention in the conflict led to honour and prestige for participants.[190] The most successful and authoritative in conflicts were the bishops of chieftainly rank due to their access to the traditional sources of authority.

---

[185] Jón Viðar Sigurðsson 1999: 87 – 88
[186] Orri Vésteinsson 1996: 164
[187] DI, no. 2
[188] Jón Viðar Sigurðsson 1999: 190
[189] Ibid, p. 213
[190] Andersson and Miller 1989: 30

b) Causing conflicts

The only conflicts set off by bishops were ones related to marital relationships, promiscuity, control of Church property and the possessions of churches. All these matters took place towards the end of the twelfth century and were posed by bishops Þorlákr Þórhallsson, Brandr Sæmundarson, and Páll Jónsson. Such a phenomenon partly exists due to a source problem – *Hungrvaka* discusses only bishops from the end of eleventh to the first half of the twelfth century; the activities of bishops of the second half of the twelfth century is better known from the detailed information in the *Sturlunga saga* compilation, *Páls saga* and *Þorláks saga*. Furthermore, conflicts, caused by bishops, were connected with the policy of the Nidaros archbishops, which came into being during the second half of the century.

The claims of the bishops were of the same nature and overall stayed within frames of the Gregorian policy. The ecclesiastical reforms started by the Benedictines of Cluny in the eleventh century and promoted by Pope Gregory VII were mainly aimed at releasing the Universal Church from the pressure of secular institutions. However, the position of the known bishops in Icelandic society was dissimilar and it led to unlike intentions and implementation of the reforms. I make a distinction between the conflicts caused by bishops with a chieftaincy – such as Brandr and Páll, and those without one – Þorlákr. What was the aim in making conflicts for the each kind of bishop? Is it possible to make any parallels with chieftains and their goals in conflicts?

The influence of Norwegian archbishop on the Icelandic Church has been mentioned above. How significant was it for Iceland? Was there any difference in the archbishop's appeals to bishop-chieftains and to Þorlákr?

Bishops of the first kind – Brandr and Páll – were hardly adherents of the ecclesiastical movement. Both were well established and had close links with the chief domineering families of Iceland. Nevertheless, there are several instances when bishops' demands were a part of the new Church policy. These were: legitimacy of marriage (one case), promiscuity (one case), and church property (one case).[191]

The outcome of the demands of Bishop Brandr concerning the legitimacy of a marriage is not known. There is information that the efforts of Bishop Páll Jónsson to separate Árni rauðskegr from his mistress Þuríðr were ineffectual.[192] Regarding two latter cases, namely inheritance of the church estate and church property, it seems likely Bishop Brandr made use of the Gregorian principles for personal purposes. A church-farm Vellir in Svarfaðardalur after the death of a priest had passed to the bishop's control. The claims on the rightful heirs to return Vellir were neglected by the bishop. Vésteinsson reasonably notes that it is questionable to what extent the accepted church law of the time

---

[191] Gsd, 9; Gsb, 17; Gsb, 11
[192] Gsb, 17

was behind Brandr in this case. It seems that the control over the estate passed to the bishop, just as it could have passed to a secular chieftain.[193] A similar situation took place in the case of church property. After the death of a priest Ingimund, the bishop announced the see of Hólar as the rightful heir of his books and vestments.

Bishops of chieftainy rank were definitely not interested in setting up *libertas ecclesiae* in Iceland. Correspondence between the chief proponent of the Gregorian reforms in Norway – Archbishop Eystein – and Iceland shows that he was well acquainted with the local political situation. What was the policy of the archbishop towards Iceland? Overall, there are four letters preserved from this correspondence. Two of them are addressed collectively to the Icelanders, the chieftains, and the bishops, and do not contain names.[194] Two others were addressed to: a) Bishop Þorlákr; and b) Bishop Þorlákr and the main chieftains of the country – Jón Loptsson, Boðvar Þórðsson, Ormr Jónsson, Oddr Gizurarson, Gizurr Hallsson.[195] Bishop Brandr is absent from the list of the receivers. Why? Sources do not provide enough information to reveal relationships between Eystein and Brandr, but it is known that they were personally connected.

Bishop Brandr participated in the coronation of King Magnus Erlingsson and the meeting of Norwegian secular and ecclesiastical leaders at Bergen in 1164, where new relationships between the Church and the State were proclaimed. Two years before (1162) Bishop Björn died and Brandr came to the archbishopric for consecration, as had each bishop-elect. The Bergen meeting had finished with the declaration of *Magnus Erlingsson's privilege letter to the church*. Archbishop Eystein Erlendsson performed the first consecration and coronation of a Norwegian king. On this occasion, Eystein obtained an oath of fidelity and obedience to the Roman Church from the boy king. King Magnus confirmed the bishop's role in the election of the king and freed Episcopal elections from the secular control.[196] Moreover, some years later, Þorgeir, a son of Bishop Brandr, stayed one winter in Norway with Archbishop Eystein.[197]

With the lack of evidence it is not possible to represent a clear picture of Eystein's influence on the Icelandic bishops. Apparently, he had links with a well-established bishop-chieftain Brandr and an adherent of the Gregorian movement Þorlákr, and worked with them to a greater or lesser degree. Similar tendencies occurred in the case of claims of Bishop Páll concerning promiscuity. Páll and Archbishop Eirik exchanged some letters;[198] and a gift-exchange took place between Páll and Archbishop Tore.[199] The policy of the archbishops made a certain impact on the bishops-chieftains.

---

[193] Órri Vésteinsson 1996: 166
[194] Reg N, no. 149, 156
[195] Reg N, no. 160, 163
[196] Lat Doc, no. 7; Johnsen 1955: 35–40; Gunnes 1996: 67–70; Helle 1964: 30–2
[197] Gsb, 11
[198] Reg N, no. 297
[199] Ps, 27

However, Brandr and Páll were rather playing with Nidaros and made quite successful attempts to get the favour of archbishops.

Noteworthy, all conflicts caused by the bishops concerned ecclesiastical matters. Hence, it can be presumed that the authority of the Church, Popes, and the Apostles gave bishops of both types a possibility to cause conflicts. The bishop-chieftains had traditional sources of authority and brought the Gregorian reforms into play much more rarely than Bishop Þorlákr.

Conflicts of Bishop Þorlákr Þórhallsson

Þorlákr was the first bishop to promote the reform programme of the Norwegian archbishops in Iceland. The episcopacy of Þorlákr and its impact on the Icelandic Church deserves a separate and thorough study; my aim here is more modest. In the focus of the present subchapter are the reasons and outcomes of conflicts caused by bishops. I will also sketch out general tendencies of the Gregorian movement in Iceland.

Þorlákr's saga narrates that his parents were "of good family and noble ancestry." It is clear that they were not prosperous and probably not influential either. When he was ordained he became a district priest in a small but profitable ministry, and his saga claims that these revenues made it possible for him to go to Paris and Lincoln. It must have been the Oddaverjar who paid for his education abroad.[200] The Oddaverjar in accordance with the Haukdælir had Þorlákr elected to the see at Skálholt. His position at the see and the bishop's authority there were undoubtedly very weak. At the beginning of Þorlákr's episcopacy Skálholt was in economical difficulties. Traditional sources of authority, such as an influential family, respected ancestry, personal wealth, etc., were not available for the bishop. Moreover, his studies in European centres made him a devotee of the church reforms. He also acknowledged Archbishop Eystein as a supreme authority and became a promoter of archbishop's policy in Iceland.

An unsolved source problem makes it difficult to examine Þorlákr's policy. There are two saga narratives about the bishop – *Þorláks saga byskups in elzta (A version)* – written around 1200 in Latin, and *Þorláks saga byskups yngri (B version or Oddaverja-þáttr)*, written in the second half of the thirteenth century in Old Norse. *Þorláks saga B* is the only source to include an account of Þorlákr's claims over church property and the date and context of its composition is disputed. Discussing the source problem Vésteinsson offers two alternatives: the first one is that *Oddaverja-þáttr* was composed as a part of the original version of *Þorláks saga* – in the first one or two decades of the thirteenth century – and that the A version is a shortened version of this original saga. If this is the case we would have to accept *Oddaverja-þáttr*'s relation of Þorlákr's challenge to the church-owners as the account of a contemporary. The other possibility is that this source was composed for propaganda

---

[200] Órri Vésteinsson, 1996: 152

purposes during Bishop Árni's conflict with the church-owners in the late thirteen century.[201] The three versions of the *Þorláks saga* have not been the subject of a detailed philological study and their relationship is therefore still ambiguous.[202] The problem with Þorlákr's claims over church property needs separate thorough examination, which will not be held in the present study.

Major topics of archiepiscopal letters to Iceland were the administration of churches and promiscuity. Eystein also prohibited clerics to bear weapons and participate in clashes, banned them from serving mass to clerics who committed murder, and remind priests about their duty to protect oppressed.[203] Central points of Þorlákr's campaign concerned church property and sexual morality. There is no independent evidence that he campaigned against clerics bearing arms.[204] The named issues conformed to the demands of Eystein according to his correspondence with Iceland.[205]

Church property

Vésteinsson argues that Þorlákr's claims on church property were misunderstood; the whole object of the exercise was the granting of the church as a fief by the bishop to the owner, but not an abdication of church property by laymen.[206] The main obstacle for the investigation of Þorlákr's claims on church property is a problem with the sources I have mentioned above. Until the source problem is solved, it does not seem possible to provide a sound explanation.

Marriage and sexual morals

Þorlákr's saga notes about the bishop's involvement into marriage issues very briefly. Following the instructions of Archbishop Eystein on the bishop's duties, Þorlákr busied himself with observing morals and broke unlawful marriages of his flock.[207] *Þorláks saga B* talks about Þorlákr's activity more explicitly. There are two cases of adultery and one case of forbidden marriage.[208]

The first two are well-known instances regarding relationships between chieftain Jón Loptsson and Ragnheiðr, chieftain Sveinn Sturlusson and his mistress. After Jón Loptsson abandoned Þorlákr's demands, no chieftain paid attention to the reformer and his campaign failed.

Þorlákr was fighting in vain. Chieftains did not obey his orders. Archbishop Eystein could not support his suffragant due to the complex political circumstances.[209] A leader of the rebels (*birkenbeinene*) – Sverre – managed to gain well-established supporters in Trøndelag and made this region a starting

---

[201] Ibid., p. 115
[202] See Órri Vésteinsson, pp. 115–21 for the full discussion of the issue
[203] Reg N, no. 149, 156, 160, 163
[204] Órri Vésteinsson 1996: 170
[205] Reg N, no. 149, 156, 160, 163
[206] Órri Vésteinsson 1996: 119
[207] Þs A, 15
[208] Þs B, 25, 26, 23
[209] Such as Sverre's revolt; Eystein's exile to England.

point for military operations. After Sverre had based himself in Nidaros, Eystein had to abandon his see and followed Magnus until the latter went into exile to England.[210] In 1181 Eystein had to go into exile to England. On return from the exile and until his death in 1188, the archbishop remained neutral and was occupied with the internal reorganization of the Church and works in Nidaros cathedral. Eystein appointed the bishop of Stavanger, Eirik Ivarsson, as his successor. Eirik was a zealous Gregorian and one of the most active supporters of King Magnus.

The third case concerns the marriage of Snælaug Högnadóttir to Þórðr Böðvarsson. She had a child before a marriage. The father of her child and her husband proved to be second cousins and "when Bishop Þorlákr learned about that, he forbade Snælaug and Þórðr to be together. But because they loved each other very much they took little notice of his sayings."[211] The bishop's verdict was clearly ignored.

Why did the lawfulness of wedlock and adultery become one of the key points of Þorlákr policy?

In his campaign, Þorlákr followed the commands of Archbishop Eystein, who in his correspondence with Iceland emphasised the misbehaviour of the Icelandic elite.[212] In addition, interference into marital issues gave the bishop economical advantages. Þorlákr imposed fines on unlawful unions and extramarital affairs. In the Christian Law Section and Betrothals Section of *Grágás* bishops are given powers to ban the adulterate[213], to incur penalties in the case of separation[214] and so on. If *Grágás*'s regulations of sex and marriage and the bishops' authority in the named issues were acknowledged, the bishops got a considerable source of income.

Moreover, interference into matrimonial questions made it possible for the bishop to have influence on many important issues – such as property, alliances and power. Families wanted to control the marriages of their offspring and the alliances formed by them. It seems that the effort of the Church to interfere with the traditional role that the family played in arranging marriages was disliked.[215]

Regarding adultery for the highborn men, extramarital affairs and a number of illegitimate children were means to gain more followers and supporters.[216] The laws gave a pivotal role to the bishops in divorce proceedings, as mediators and final arbitrators over people's private lives.[217] In theory such a control would increase the political influence of a bishop.

---

[210] Helle 1964: 55
[211] Þs B, 23
[212] Reg N, no. 163
[213] Grg I, K 1
[214] Grg II, K 149
[215] Korpiola 1999: 133, 139
[216] Orri Vésteinsson 1996: 172 in notes
[217] Ibid, p. 171

For better understanding of the phenomenon of bishops causing conflicts, I shall compare it with the situation among the secular powers. The farmers usually asked the chieftains for support in legal cases. The chieftain's supremacy when it came to the legal decisions forced all the farmers to become the clients of a chieftain. He alone was in a position to help, whether as defendant or plaintiff.[218] A successfully resolved disagreement made a considerable investment into a chieftain's prestige and honour. In other words, the ability to settle lawsuits was a part of the power base of the chieftains. However, not only resolving conflicts was important. In order to get more power and establish one's position among the leaders and farmers, the chieftains played on the antagonism that existed in society. Examples are numerous, the most representative one – a feud between Sturla and Einarr.[219] In conditions of limited resources of the country only the chieftains had enough means and power to participate in the political game.

As a part of the aristocratic network of the island, Icelandic bishops participated in the major conflicts of the country. Nevertheless, bishops by both types could cause conflicts only in ecclesiastical matters. In part, it occurred due to the fact that the office was fixed and lifelong, so there was no need to fight for supporters and represent their interests, as did chieftains. Moreover, Christianity provided the bishops with a new kind of authority, based on the spiritual power of the Church, the Popes, and the Apostles; and gave them the potential to cause conflicts. Bishop-chieftains had traditional sources of authority and brought the Gregorian reforms into play much more rarely than Bishop Þorlákr. Brandr and Páll used a new trend for personal benefits and as a concession to the archbishop's policy. Bishop Þorlákr lacked the authority other than the one of the Church. He made an attempt to gain an influence in fields extremely significant for the chieftains' power.

---

[218] Jón Viðar Sigurðsson 1999: 214
[219] HSs

Chapter 3. Other tasks

Attention to the law issues in the sagas make us to think that the law and legality played a momentous role in Icelandic society. Miller argues: "Iceland developed a legal system – courts, experts in law, rules clearly articulated as laws – in the absence of any coercive state institutions."[220] Byock underlines that "in Iceland the cultural focus was on law. The relationship with a godi and his followers was set by the law."[221] However, a closer examination reveals that in practice courts hardly made a decision whether a person was guilty or not. Due to such peculiarity of juridical system, it was more important to settle a dispute through a direct agreement and arbitrage. Throughout the sagas, men with a good knowledge of the law are greatly respected but there is only occasionally any indication that it was important to respect the law.[222] The reason why legal cases and arbitration were so important lies in field of profit – fines and goods confiscated during successful cases were important sources of wealth for the Icelandic elites.[223] Olason emphasizes: "success of the thing and the keeping peace was dependent of the grace of the gods in whose name the Thing is hallowed."[224] Function of *alþingi* as a meeting place for chieftains and members of their families was not least important than its juridical function. In a society where manifestation of wealth played crucial role for men in power, public meetings palayed a significant role.

Despite the diversity of opinions concerning the role of law in Iceland, laws were certainly important. The legislation function of the Law Council gave the chieftains prestige and status. Legislation and codes of law containing Icelandic and often translations of foreign law, too, indicated the unique position of the chieftains in society.[225] Christian culture provided the means and even some of the models for writing the laws; there were already extensive laws available to be transcribed well before the advent of Christianity.[226] What was the role of the bishops in the lawmaking process in Iceland?

Distinctive feature of Icelandic medieval culture was co-existence and interweaving of local, oral, prechristian elements with continental, written and Christian elements. The crossroad of these two currents was centres of learning and literary activity of the country – schools. The second subchapter aims to characterize the educational activity of the bishops, such as the foundation of schools and teaching. For a better understanding of the education process in Iceland, I briefly discuss the European model.

---

[220] Miller 1990: 224
[221] Byock 1990: 7
[222] Sigurdsson 1999 : 173, 175–6
[223] Smith, Parsons 1989 : 183
[224] Olason 2000 : 134
[225] Jón Viðar Sigurðsson 1999: 178
[226] Foote 1984: 155–64

a) Lawmaking

There is a twofold division in the lawmaking activity of the Icelandic bishops: promotion of the Tithe Law and enactment of the Christian Law.

The Tithe Law was instituted in 1096 or 1097 at the Alþingi.[227] The initiative of Bishop Gizurr was profitable for the Icelandic elite, which unsurprisingly supported the enactment of the new law. The body of laws has been handed down in many manuscripts, of which the Codex Regius of *Grágás* supposedly a mid-thirteenth century manuscript, is the oldest. Jóhannesson argues that the Tithe Law was written down in the twelfth century. The rules on tithe payment were included in the Code of Church Law. To his point of view, this inclusion would have been unnecessary if the recording of the entire Tithe Law preceded that of the Code of Church Law.[228]

Among all Scandinavian countries, it was the first successful example of introducing the tithe. In Norway the tithe system was not made law until the 1120s or 1130s, and then only in parts of the country.[229]

The Icelandic tithe was a one per cent property tax; the rationale being that as standard interest was ten per cent, one per cent of property would equal ten per cent of potential yields. *Hungrvaka* claims that a fourfold division – church, priest, bishop, and the poor – was original. In fact, there were some particularities in this division. Priests were not direct recipients of any part of the tithes; instead, tithes were placed in the custody of churchwardens. The bishop decided to which church the tithe of each farmstead should go.[230] The bishop's part of the tithe and his influence on the church-part were considerable powers but they didn't allow the bishops any more influence over the tithe payments. Half of the tithe was payable to the churches and all churches were privately owned. It is reasonable to assume that the church-owners were among the richest and most powerful in society, they were those who controlled legislation at the Alþingi. It was clearly to their advantage to let such a law be passed.[231] Part of the tithe for the poor was distributed in territorial unit called *hreppar*. *Hreppar* were communal units; one of the essential functions of them was to support their residents and to provide relief for the poor. There is reliable evidence that such units existed at the time of the introducing of the Tithe Law in 1097.[232]

Most of the scholars point to the immense importance of the Tithe Law for the Icelandic Church.[233] Jóhannesson underlines that this law "made the Church independent and laid down the

---

[227] Hungrvaka, 5
[228] Jón Jóhannesson 1974: 171
[229] Helle 1964: 41, 167
[230] Jón Jóhannesson 1974: 175
[231] Orri Vesteinsson 1996: 69
[232] Jón Jóhannesson 1974: 83–4, 86
[233] Magnús Már Lárusson 1965; Sigurður Nordal 1990; Jón Jóhannesson 1974

foundation for its wealth."[234] It should be remembered that the Law itself could not make the Church financially independent; there were no executive authorities in the country and the Church was not an autonomous institution. However, the law was lucrative for the entire circle of ecclesiastical-secular elite and became an economic base for the growth of wealth and power of the aristocratic families.

In Europe, a fight between the secular and ecclesiastical authorities for the tithe was a big issue. At first, the tithe was payable to a bishop, later the right passed by common law to the parish priests. The right to receive tithes was also granted to princes and nobles, even hereditarily, by ecclesiastics in return for protection or services, and this type of impropriation became so intolerable that the Third Lateran Council (1179) decreed that no alienation of tithes might gain consent of the pope.[235]

The most important achievement in the field of lawmaking was the initiative of the bishops Þorlákr Runólfsson and Ketill Þorsteinsson to write down the Christian Law (*kristinn réttr*) "according to the observations of the wisest men and by advice of Archbishop Özurr."[236] The Christian Law section of the law codex *Grágás* lays down rules concerning burials, baptism, church affairs, mass days, offices of bishops and priests, feast days, fasting, heresy and so on. The codification of the Christian laws occurred shortly after the revision and recording of the secular laws in 1117–18 and might be influenced by the feud between the chieftains Þorgils and Hafliði, which was discussed earlier. Jóhannesson argues that the codification took place in 1123, after Bishop Ketill returned from his consecration.[237]

In the diocese of Skálholt the Code of Church Law remained in force until 1275, when the code of Bishop Árni Þorláksson was adopted. But in the diocese of Hólar it was abrogated by royal decree on October 19, 1354.[238] The Code forms the first chapter of *Grágás*. However, the two main manuscripts of *Grágás* – *Konungsbók* and *Staðarhólsbók* – were written down in the middle of thirteenth century and around 1270 respectively.[239] Therefore, it does not seem possible to distinguish amendments which were made in the code throughout the centuries to the original text of 1123.

Did the codification of the laws bring any alterations to the bishops' position in society? The Christian Law section of *Grágás* is a short guidebook for laymen on how to practise Christianity. Concerning bishops' power *Grágás* regards only the division of the country into two bishoprics, the bishop's duties such as visitation of dioceses, the consecration of churches, the payment of bishop's tithes, and the bishop's agents.[240] The priests' section adds to the list the clauses on priests' obedience

---

[234] Jón Jóhannesson 1974: 149
[235] www.newadvent.org
[236] Hungrvaka, 6
[237] Jón Jóhannesson 1974: 161
[238] Ibid.
[239] Grg, I, pp. 1–21
[240] Grg I, K 5

to their bishop and on the court of the priests.[241] The regulations themselves do not indicate much about the power of Icelandic bishops. However, it should not be forgotten that legislative activity signalled the power of the bishop and was meaningful for the chieftains who used the same means to draw a line between them and society.[242]

The Law Council section of *Grágás* contains an important passage about the bishops' manuscripts of the secular code. "It is also prescribed that in this country what is found in books is to be law. And if books differ, then that is found in the books, which the bishops own is to be accepted. If their books also differ, then that one is to prevail which says it at greater length in words that affect the case at issue. But if they say it at the same length but each in its own version, then the one, which is in Skálholt, is to prevail. Everything in the book which Hafliði had made is to be accepted unless it has since been modified, but only those things in the accounts given by other legal experts which do not contradict it, though anything in them which supplies what is left out there or is to be accepted."[243] Hafliði Másson had close links with both sees.[244] Before the arrival of Christianity, the laws were transmitted orally. The power and prestige of the lawspeaker was based not on a book, as it happened within the Church, but on knowledge that the lawspeaker had had to acquire from the lips of other wise men. It should be underlined that a working knowledge of the law was essential to every chieftain who engaged in litigation.[245] The passage from the Law Council section is a representative example of long process of transmission from an oral to a written legal culture. Hafliði attempted to fix the knowledge and authority of the lawspeaker in the written book. In his attempt Hafliði tried to empower the leaders of the Christian Church with the highest authority in disputes of law.

Actually, nothing suggests that it would have worked out that way in practice. The law manuscripts were private law books. Nobody had a monopoly when it came to recording laws in writing. Private notation on some scale doubtlessly took place before 1117 and certainly did so thereafter.[246]

Interestingly, it was not until the twelfth century, when the Church had become genuinely powerful – see as a witness the huge cathedral consecrated at Skálholt shortly after the middle of that century – that a priestly member of the Haukdælir family, Gizurr Hallsson, was appointed to the secular office of lawspeaker.[247]

---

[241] Grg I, K 6
[242] Jón Viðar Sigurðsson 1999: 177
[243] Grg I, K 117
[244] Bishop-elect of Skálholt Hallr Teitsson was Hafliði's cousin in law; his sister was a second wife of Hafliði. The bishop of Skálholt Þorlákr and the bishop of Hólar Ketill were related to Hallr and, therefore, through Hallr to Hafliði. Besides, Þorlákr's brother in law was a father of Hallr – Teitr Ísleifsson they were both adopted by Hallr Þórarinsson in Haukdælir.
[245] Jón Viðar Sigurðsson 2004: 57
[246] Grg I, pp. 10–11
[247] Jón Viðar Sigurðsson 2004: 61

Since the two Icelandic bishops were members of the Court of Legislature Jóhannesson argues that they could freely exercise their influence upon lawmaking at the Alþingi.[248] It is hard to agree with this statement; hardly, bishops were independent political players. It was already pointed out above the bishop's position in the aristocratic network depended on the authority of his family. Even the most powerful bishops were connected to chieftains by links of family or friendship.

Theoretically, the Icelandic Church as a branch of the Roman Catholic Church was under Canon Law. Canon Law is the body of laws and regulations made by, or adopted by, ecclesiastical authority for the government of the Christian organization and its members.[249] I have not met any indication in my material that the Canon Law was implemented in Iceland. Attempts to separate clerical jurisdiction from secular and subordinate Icelandic clergy to the regulations of the Catholic Church in practice took place towards the end of the twelfth century and occurred under the pressure of the Nidaros archbishop.

Generally speaking, knowledge of the laws was highly respected in Iceland. It marked one's position in society. For the chieftains training in law was important due to their activity in prosecuting and defending claims on behalf of their supporters. A chieftain, without skill in law, was considered worthy of mention.[250] *Hungrvaka* highly praised bishops who were knowledgeable in laws and capable in speeches.[251] Indeed, legislative activity indicated authority. However, on only one occasion did the bishops create and implement a law – the Tithe Law. Writing down the Christian Law section should be seen in the light of the transmission from an oral to a written legal culture. Codification of the Christian laws was closely connected to the recording of the secular laws and particularly the attempts of Hafliði Másson to monopolize legislation.

b) Education

It is known that two schools existed under patronage of bishops – at Skálholt and at Hólar. Unfortunately, a detailed account concerns only the Hólar School.

It seems quite possible that the first Icelandic bishop – Ísleifr was educated abroad at the cloister Herford in Westphalia, Saxony, which accepted only nuns of high birth.[252] Stay at Herford of his son, Gizurr, is less certain. Ísleifr was not the only bishop in eleventh century Iceland; there were

---

[248] Jón Jóhannesson 1974: 164
[249] www.newadvent.org/canon law
[250] HSs, 6
[251] Hungrvaka, 6, 8
[252] He appeared at Herford due to his family connections. An abbess of the monastery – Godesthi – was the aunt of Duke Ordulfr, who was married to Ulfhildr, the daughter of St. Olaf. Hallr Þórarinsson – a foster father of Ísleifr's son Teitr – was a retainer of St. Olaf.

missionary bishops as well, who must have trained youths. According to *Hungrvaka* many men sent their sons to Ísleifr for education.[253] Proceeding from the passage of Ari the Learned (ch. 9) about the bishop and also from the similar account in *Jóns saga Helga* (ch. 3) Jóhannesson presumes that it was Ísleifr, who founded the school at Skálholt.[254] However, it is necessary at first to define what kind of school existed at Skálholt.

Education in the family (in a form of fosterage) and on a school bench are dissimilar phenomena. The former came about orally by learning poetry, stories, and ancient knowledge. One of the main aims of fosterage was to create alliances and settle strong personal connections and loyalty between a foster child and a foster family.[255]

In Europe, education took place in monasteries or cathedral schools, which definitely lacked a family atmosphere. In the monasteries of Anglo-Saxon England, and in the Benedictine houses of the Norman era, education was provided within the monastery for both oblates and for outsiders. But such cases were not common, and education for the laity was more likely to be provided by schools run under the auspices of the religious houses and staffed by secular masters, rather than at the monasteries themselves.[256] On the continent, schools did not normally admit pupils from outside. The *Capitula of Aachen* (817), which asserted the authority of the Rule of St. Benedict for all the monks of the Carolingian Empire, even forbade monks to teach all except oblates. Charlemagne put education as a duty upon the secular clergy.[257]

There is not enough information to depict the form of education at Skálholt School; however, it seems to be based on a traditional way of transmitting of knowledge from a father to a son. Some of Ísleifr's pupils later became important clerics, and two of them were bishops: St. Jón and also Kollr, bishop of the people of Vík.[258]

There is a more detailed description of the Hólar School, founded by Bishop Jón. Although, Jón's disciples could be his foster sons, teaching at Hólar looks similar to the European pattern. Jón brought to the school two foreign teachers, one of whom was Gísli a son of Finni from Gautland, who was to teach priestlings and sermons, and another, a Frenchmen Rikini.[259] The school at Hólar became an important establishment for education (especially learning Latin) and writing.

Interestingly, almost all the bishops and some abbots got their education in one of these two schools. The bishop of Skálholt Klængr Þorsteinsson, Bishop Björn Gilsson of Hólar, Vilmundr, the first abbot of Þingeyrar, abbot of Hitardalur, Hrein. At Skálholt – bishops Jón Ögmundarson and Björn

---

[253] Hungrvaka, 2
[254] Jón Jóhannesson 1974: 146
[255] Nygård 1997: 31, Jón Viðar Sigurðsson 1999: 144
[256] Burton 1995: 188, 189
[257] Knowles 1963: 26
[258] Jsh, 3
[259] Jsh, 11

Gilsson studied at Hólar. The exceptions were four bishops of Skálholt: three bishop-chieftains of the Haukdælir family (Ísleifr, Gizurr, and Páll) and a bishop without significant family links but under the control of the Haukdælir – Þorlákr Þórhallsson who studied abroad. It does not seem that education in the European universities had influence on the bishops' policies in Iceland, since the representatives of the two different types – with and without a chieftaincy – studied abroad. The bishops' policies were still dependent on their position in the aristocratic network.

In general, teaching was tremendously respected in Iceland. Distinguished teachers were in great demand.[260] Education was one of the bishops' duties. Bishops Þorlákr and Klængr are said to have pupils. Þorlákr "took a lot of men for teaching and made them good scholars [*kennar*: also a teacher, a priest] ... and in many ways he strengthened Christianity in Iceland."[261]

In Iceland, secular and religious teaching was more intermingled than in Europe. Bishop Ísleifr educated the sons of the chieftains as well as clergy. The schools at Skálholt and Hólar, headed by the bishops, were important centres of learning where the traditional pattern of oral transmission of knowledge was combined with the Christian one based on a book. It is known that the Hólar School had more European features than the school at Skálholt.

Schools at the sees were not the only educational centres in Iceland. At Haukdælir, another school under the priest Teitr – a brother of Bishop Gizurr – was organized; he fostered and taught many clerics, and two of his pupils became bishops: bishops Þorlákr the first and Björn."[262] Teitr got his knowledge from his foster father Hallr of Haukdælir. Teitr was not only a priest, and learned in clerical arts; he is also remembered as an authority on the history of Iceland, on the settlement, the pagan laws, and the Conversion.[263] There was a school at Oddi founded by Sæmundr the Wise (1056) which supposed to be a secular one. Unfortunately, there is the only information about this school.

In the eleventh to twelfth centuries the Icelandic clerical elite was wedded with the top of the secular hierarchy. Bishops were a part of the secular-ecclesiastical network, which on the whole was interested in knowledge.

In the table below I present bishops and places of their studies:

---

[260] HSs, 34
[261] Hungrvaka, 6
[262] Jsh, 3
[263] Turville-Petre 1953: 78

Skálholt:

Name:	Studied at:
Ísleifr Gizurarson 1056–80	Monastery Herford, Saxony
Gizurr Ísleifsson 1082–1118	Monastery Herford, Saxony
Þorlákr Runólfsson 1118–33	Haukdælir
Magnús Einarsson 1134–48	No information
Hallr Teitsson d.1148	Haukdælir
Klængr Þorsteinsson 1152–76	St. Jón's school at Hólar
Þorlákr Þórhallsson 1178–93	Paris and Lincoln
Páll Jónsson 1195–1211	Abroad

Hólar:

Name:	Studied at:
Jón Ögmundson 1106–21	Skálholt school
Ketill Þorsteinsson 1122–45	No information
Björn Gilsson 1147–62	Haukdælir, Hólar school
Brandr Sæmundson 1163–1201	No information

Chapter 4. Icelandic pattern of bishop's office in European context

In the present chapter, the Icelandic pattern of the bishop's office is viewed in a European context. What were the duties of a bishop according to the regulations of the Christian Church? What were actual tasks of bishops? Evidently, the pattern changed from country to country; for that reason, under consideration will be the countries, which were ecclesiastically and culturally connected to Iceland – Germany, Denmark and Norway. Due to the differences in source material concerning the bishop's office in the named countries, I cannot investigate tasks of the bishops in the named countries in the same way as it was done on the Icelandic material.

The second subchapter aims to examine the influence of the Gregorian reform on Iceland in the light of Icelandic relationships with Norway.

a) Duties of bishop according to Christian regulations

The bishop – is the title of the ecclesiastical dignitary who possesses the fullness of the priesthood to rule a diocese as its chief pastor, in due submission to the primacy of the Pope. They are appointed for the government of one portion of the faithful of the Church, under the direction and authority of the sovereign pontiff. They are the successors of the Apostles, though they do not possess all the prerogatives of the latter.[264]

Although, the *Gospels* do not provide an accurate description of the office, they do present certain rights and authorities, which became a foundation of the development of characterization.

The rights and powers of the bishops were developing since the establishment of the office. Theoretically, a bishop had the powers of order and jurisdiction. The power of order comes to him through his Episcopal consecration, but the exercise of this right depends on his power of jurisdiction.

The following functions are reserved to the bishop: the dedication of a church, the consecration of an altar, of chalices and patens, and generally of the articles serving for the celebration of Holy Mass, the reconciliation of a desecrated church, the benediction of bells, the benediction of an abbot, the benediction of the holy oils, etc.

The power of jurisdiction gives bishops the right to prescribe for the faithful the rules, which the latter must follow. The power of jurisdiction is of Divine origin in the sense that the Pope is held to establish in the Church bishops whose mission it is to direct the faithful in the way of salvation. The bishops then have in their dioceses an ordinary jurisdiction, limited, however, by the rights that the Pope can reserve to himself in virtue of his primacy. With their consecration, bishops acquired the

---

[264] This definition was formulated at the Council of Trent (13.12.1545–4.12.1563) in the document Council of Trent, Sess. XXIII, ch. iv; can. vi, vii. Source: www.newadvent.org

authority to punish people for acts of disobedience by imposing an interdict or excommunication upon them.

Among the authorities of the bishop are teaching (the right to teach Christian doctrine) and governing (includes legislative, judicial, coercive, and administrative powers).

A bishop possesses certain obligations: to preserve the true faith and a high moral tone among the people; to be a good example, by preaching; to perform the good administration of the diocese; to educate youth; to train his clergy. The Church has imposed as special obligations upon bishops the canonical visitation of the diocese and the holding of an annual diocesan synod; a bishop has also obligations regarding the Holy See: to visit the shrines of Sts. Peter and Paul at Rome and present a report on the condition of his diocese. In the time of Paschal II (1099–1118), only metropolitans were bound to pay this visit.[265]

To exercise its rights and powers each office normally needs commonly recognized regulations or laws. The problem with authorities of bishops in medieval Europe is the absence of a centralized canon law or universally accepted collection of such laws. The Gregorian reform, which started in the middle of the eleventh century, intended to strengthen the Church as an organization, to build up the complete body of church laws and to create a mechanism of control and punishment. Ecumenical councils of the twelfth century were set (among other issues) to clarify the position of bishops in the church hierarchy, the extent of their powers and their jurisdiction. The central issue was the land property of the church and the right to appoint in office – the *beneficiaries*. At the start of the Gregorian reform the chief factor in the control of a parish church was not the authority of the bishop, but that of the secular lord, sometimes the bishop, sometimes the clerk by virtue of his office in the Episcopal curia or a cathedral or a collegiate church, sometimes a religious house, but generally a layman. The aim of papal legislation from Urban II (1088–99) onwards was to place parish churches under the authority of the bishop.

The first Lateran Council (1123) decreed that a priest was not to become a priest of a particular church either by investiture at the hands of the secular lord or by hereditary right, but through being constituted a priest of that church by a bishop.[266]

A significant stage in defining the authorities and powers of bishops was the *Concordantia discordantium canonum*, known later as *Decretum*, published at Bologna about 1148 by a teacher of canon law – Gratian. The first part forms an introduction to the general principles of the Canon Law; the second part discusses of ecclesiastical administration and marriage; the third part treats of the sacraments and other sacred things.[267]

---

[265] www.newadvent.org; KLNM, I: Biskop
[266] Addleshaw 1956: 4,17
[267] www.newadvent.org

The main issue in the Second Lateran Council (1139) was the election of the bishop. Pope Innocent II confined the privilege of electing the bishop to the cathedral chapter and the representatives of the regular clergy, and made no mention of lay participation in the election. The ecclesiastical party assumed that this provision annulled the king's participation in elections and his right to decide in the case of an equally divided vote of the electors.[268]

The Third Lateran Council (1179) forbade promoting anyone to the episcopate before the age of thirty or of illegitimate birth. A candidate must have spent a certain period in priest's orders and be of good character and sound doctrine.[269]

Pope Alexander III (1159–81) maintained that the relationships between a secular lord and his church should be thought of in terms not of dominium, but of *jus patronatus* ('just or good patronage'). *Jus patronatus* is a right not of giving a church to a clerk but, but of presenting a church to a bishop, to whom the actual giving of the church belongs owing to its spiritual nature. It brought to an end some of the abuses of the proprietary church system.[270]

Subsequently, the Council of Trent (1545–63) defined the rights of the bishop. A reform, treating of the mode of life of the cardinals and the bishops, the certificates of fitness for ecclesiastics, the legacies for Masses, the administration of ecclesiastical benefices, the suppression of concubinage among the clergy, and the life of the clergy in general was approved.

b) Bishop's office in Germany, Denmark, Norway

Germany

In the eleventh century the perception of the office of bishop, the extent of his powers and authorities was not fully established. A number of studies dealing with bishops in the eleventh century underlines that there was a certain view on the bishop's office.[271]

Timothy Reuter highlights that we are dealing with the ascribed rather than the achieved status.[272] Sean Gilsdorf underlines the role of bishop as a mediator.[273] The theological foundation for Episcopal peacemaking was provided by Christ's declaration in the Beatitudes (Matthew 5: 9): "Blessed are the peacemakers, for they shall see God."[274] Central to Episcopal peacemaking was the practice of mediation and arbitration. However, Episcopal mediation should not be understood in terms of "neutrality", but rather as a complex political act. The bishop's role and image as mediator

---

[268] www.newadvent.org
[269] The Oxford dictionary of the Christian Church 1990: 179
[270] Addleshaw 1956: 18
[271] Bourchard 2004; Gilsdorf 2004; Jaeger 1983; Parisse 2004; Reuter 2004
[272] Reuter 2004: 34
[273] Gilsdorf 2004: 55–6
[274] www.newadvent.org: Bishop

and intercessor in the late Carolingian and Ottonian world resonated with a broader conception of the *bishop-sacerdos* as a mediating figure between heaven and earth.[275]

The Roman law assigns the bishops the role of protectors of the weak and oppressed.[276] This patron-role of bishop cannot be separated from his function as intercessor. In many cases the person for whom a bishop interceded was bound to him by affective or official ties – as his cleric, his suffragan, his relative, or his ally.[277]

Michel Parisse talks about the pastoral functions of bishop: his responsibility for faith and dogma, and thus for the moral health and future salvation of his flock. As the head of Christendom, the bishop became the sole judge for everything touching on religion and on membership in the Church. The bishop judged behaviour, determined the rules that had to be followed, and intervened in social matters.[278]

In Europe before the Investiture struggle, the prerogatives of the Episcopal office could scarcely be described without constant reference to its secular role and to the powers, which monarchs delegated to the bishops.[279] The bishops in the Ottonian Empire exercised a central role in the administration system. They got much power from the emperors and were authoritative and loyal to the emperors.[280] At the same time, with very few exceptions, the German bishops were entirely under the control of sovereignty. This was the case with regards to their election, the confirmation of those elections, and their service to the king.[281]

C. Stephen Jaeger in his study of the bishops of the Ottonian Empire demonstrates that the political role of the imperial bishop was first and foremost as an administrator, statesman, and diplomat. Piety was not a requisite quality for the position in the same way that statesmanship and administrative skills were.[282]

Before the reformation movement had started during the papacy of Leo IX, the role of bishop was to supervise religion and be of assistance to princes. The bishops were closely connected to high secular power and were themselves powerful and wealthy noblemen who had no real head in ecclesiastical matters. German bishops together with secular magnates participated in the elections of the emperor of the Holy Roman Empire. The leading role in this process in the first half of the twelfth century belonged to the archbishop of Mainz.[283] A representative example is Hugh, the bishop of Auxerre (Burgundy) in the first part of eleventh century. He was both lifelong churchman and

---

[275] Gilsdor 2004: 57, 73
[276] www.newadvent.org: bishop; KLNM, I: Biskop
[277] Gilsdorf 2004: 67
[278] Parisse 2004: 8–15
[279] Benson 1968: 377
[280] Gunnes 1996: 52
[281] Parisse 2004: 17
[282] Jaeger 1983: 293–4
[283] Arnold 2004: 384

powerful noble. Noteworthy is that his powerful position in the secular world was instrumental in establishing a kind of monastic reform.[284]

Denmark

The first bishops in Denmark were missionaries and got their powers from the kings and the *þing*. The new Danish church was subordinated under the archbishop of Hamburg-Bremen, although the kings wanted a more independent church. When Sven Forkbeard and his son Cnut (1013–35) conquered England, the German influence was replaced with that of the Anglo-Saxon Church. Subsequently, bishops became influential governors who formed the political ideology. Practically, their tasks during this period lay in the field of supervision of the king's lands. According to tradition, King Cnut tried to introduce some sort of ecclesiastic jurisdiction and probably tithes too. The bishop of Jutland, Odinkar, set up the first taxation in the region, built churches and tried to organize the governing of his territory. Later, with the establishment of the ecclesiastical territorial division, Jutland diocese was based on the old system of *syssel*.

The growing tension between the Danish king and the German emperors made the subordination of the Danish bishops under the archbishop of Hamburg-Bremen intolerable. As several popes were sympathetic to any curtailment of imperial sovereignty, a Danish province was established in 1104 with Lund as the metropolitan centre originally for all Scandinavia but then just Denmark after the Norwegian province was founded in 1152 in Nidaros and the Swedish province in 1164 in Uppsala. The growing international influence on the Danish church resulted in an attempt to enforce celibacy, and, in the Gregorian tradition, many leading churchmen claimed total immunity from secular interference. In the middle of the twelfth century cathedral chapters came into existence (for example Ribe in 1145), and they initially wavered between a regular and a secular organization.

During the twelfth century the Danish bishops were becoming more and more powerful. They possessed a large amount of landholdings, had a military retinue, and could mobilize the entire army (*leidang*) of the region. Moreover, they were immune from taxation by the king's privilege. Towards the end of the twelfth century they got the right to mint coins. Bishops participated in clashes between the king and the aristocracy on the side of the latter.[285]

---

[284] Bourchard 2004: 43–5
[285] KLNM I, 622. It should be added that conflicts in the High Middle Ages between Church and state ended in a theoretical victory for the Church. But in its struggles for immunities and independence from the secular powers, the Danish church had become increasingly dependent upon Rome. Instead of royal taxes, the bishops had to pay considerable amounts of payments for papal confirmation. The popes interfered in Episcopal elections; claimed rights of provision, and through appeals to Curia made their power felt in everyday life. Especially unpopular were numerous papal crusade taxes; and since the fourteenth century was filled with crises, warfare, and civil war, culminating in an interregnum in Denmark in 1332–40.

Norway

During the early period, the bishops did not stay in a constant place and had to follow the kings. Snorri describes a bishop as an indefeasible part of the king's personal retinue (*hirð*).[286] The appointing of bishops into office was completely dependent on the king. Churches were privately owned and bishops had no rights to appoint priests. The farmers influenced the appointment of priests, who were gradually recruited from the local community and attached to it through marriage. Gradually local churches came under the control of bishops. Nevertheless, when it comes to the public assembles and legislation the situation was a little different. The bishops had an influence on folk assemblies and lawmaking processes there.[287] The provincial laws included the special Church laws with provisions governing the relationship between a church and people.

From Olaf Kyrre's time onwards, the role which the king played in legal issues in the public assembles crossed over to the bishop. The latter got juridical competence in his district and in many cases took the initiative to push Christian laws. Later, in assemblies, bishops acted as a kind of "law consultant" in the same position as king. Although the oldest laws (Borgathing laws) declared that the bishop should have a meeting in the *þing* with officials in order to "fight for Christian laws", the bishop did not have any juridical privileges. However, together with his function as a representative of supreme authority he got the possibility to fulfil the interests of the Church. A bishop had the authority to supervise religious matters. Apart from the abovementioned cases, the Norwegian bishop had commonly recognized ecclesiastical functions: to ordain priests and abbots, to consecrate churches, churchyards, and inventories, to bless the sacraments which were not allowed to a priest, to strengthen Christian faith, and to observe priests.[288]

c) Influence of Gregorian reform on Iceland

The reform movement which started in the middle of the eleventh century was mainly intended on liberation the Universal Church from the secular control. Until the middle of the twelfth century the Gregorian reform did not reach Iceland. The reason was distance and difficulties with transportation on the island, and furthermore the still loose organization of the Catholic Church itself, and the ambiguousness in its powers and authorities, and the absence of economical and political interest towards Iceland.

The Norwegian period of the Icelandic Church was marked by slow drift of Icelandic clergy towards the *libertas ecclesiae*. The Gregorian reform was implemented in Norway by archbishop

---

[286] Heimskringla
[287] KLNM I, 620
[288] Oftested, Rasmussen, and Schumacher 1991: 37

Eystein. The foundation of the archbishopric at Nidaros is explored by a number of studies; and for this reason, it will not be discussed here.[289] The focus question in the present subchapter is the implementation of the Gregorian reform in Norway and its impact on Iceland.

The correspondence between the Pope and Archbishop Eystein in 1169–73 shows that Eystein was working hard to clarify the issues of church organization and rights.[290] The archbishop became a decisive figure in the elections of bishops. The Pope's letter of 1169 empowered the archbishop of Trondheim to appoint a new bishop of Oslo to fill the office of a murdered predecessor.[291] In his response letters in 1160s to the archbishop the Pope again and again underlined a ban on lay investiture. Liberation (juridical) from secular influence on ecclesiastical elections led to a reinforcement of the Church as an organization headed by the Pope. Already at the coronation of Pope Adrian IV, due emphasis was laid on the monarchic function of the Pope.[292] Presumably, it was universally accepted that the Pope has a right to intervene in the bishop's elections if there were disagreements in candidacy.[293] Papal policy was aimed to provide the Universal Church with strict hierarchical structure. One of the possibilities to do it, was the unification of norms and practises of the church's life. Pope Alexander III (1159–81) enlarged the privileges of archbishop: he ordered bishops to compensate the archbishop of Nidaros for the visitation of dioceses, and to pay the metropolitan when he visited Rome.[294] Certain matters concerning rights and duties of the archbishop were still unclear[295], but the papacy in several instances during the late twelfth and early thirteenth centuries recognized the archbishop's jurisdictional overlordship over his province's bishops and their subjects.[296]

The requests of Archbishop Eystein towards Iceland which were issued in 1173–79 were aimed to draw a line between clerical and lay orders.[297] It was not an elaborated reform program; nonetheless, it concerned the main issues on the agenda of the Catholic Church.[298] Bishop Þorlákr became a supporter of archbishop's policy in Iceland and a promoter of Gregorian reform. In his campaign Þorlákr concentrated on marriage, concubinage, and the possession of church issues. It should be noted here that the well-established bishops Brandr and Páll also raised questions of marriage, promiscuity, and church property. The nature of these cases was discussed above.

---

[289] Joys 1948; Johnsen 1945, 1955, 2003; Gunnes 1996; Helle; 1964
[290] Reg N, no. 127 – 144
[291] Reg N, no. 131
[292] Ullman 1976: 233–52
[293] Joys 1948: 150
[294] Lat Doc, no. 20, 21
[295] Such as consecration of newly elected suffragans, preaching, and visitation.
[296] Perron 2003: 13
[297] Reg N, no. 149, 156, 159, 160, 163
[298] Marriage and promiscuity matters, injustice and violence against clerics, lay investiture, duties and way of conduct of clergy.

What was the Church policy towards marriage and concubinage during the period under consideration? Among the regulations of the Catholic Church were several canonical impediments that prevented a couple from marrying each other. The most important were:

a) Too close kinship, consanguinity. At first relationships were forbidden between relatives until the seventh degree, but the Fourth Lateran Council (1215) cut short the regulation until the fourth degree.

b) Affinity. It forbade marriages between spouses, who were too closely connected by marriage or a sexual relationship between their relatives.

c) Spiritual affinity. It prohibited a person from marrying his or her godchild, godfather, or their close relatives.[299]

Control over marriages gave the Church a considerable degree of political influence. Most aristocracy was related within the seventh degree. This control allowed the aristocratic authorities – in practice the Pope, if the marriage involved kings – to intervene at will to bind or to loosen, and so dominate the political scene.[300]

Interestingly, both cases of extramarital affairs which Þorlákr fought against concerned influential chieftains. In Europe, lay concubinage persisted through out the Middle Ages. It was not until the Reformation period that concubinage among the laity was finally and definitely prohibited by the Church.[301]

European ecclesiastics disapproved of concubinage on moral grounds. However, a well-defined pattern of marriage was still absent. The base collection of the medieval canon law – *Decretum Gratianum* – contains a canon, which witnesses that concubinage was tolerated by the Church and that it might in fact be considered the functional equivalent of marriage. The author of the *Decretum* – Gratian – apparently concluded that marriage and concubinage, although different in some legal effects, were nonetheless essentially the same.[302]

King Sverre Sigurdsson strove to recover control over the election of bishops and ecclesiastical property. Archbishop Eirik (1189–1205) and his successor Tore (1206–14) had personal connections with a group of clergy, which had its centre in St. Victor monastery in Paris, the original reform centre. An open struggle between the king and the archbishops started almost immediately after the appointment of Eirik. In 1190, Eirik was driven into exile. He appealed to Rome against the usurpation and the attack on the Church's rights. In 1193 Celestine III's sentence of excommunication against the king and his adherents unleashed a lingering resistance between *regnum* and *sacerdotium*.

---

[299] Korpiola 1999: 153–4
[300] Duby 1997: 9
[301] Brundage 1975: 10
[302] Brundage 1975: 4–5

Despite his unstable position, Archbishop Eirik demonstrated a certain amount of interest in the situation of the Icelandic Church. His two letters issued in 1189 concerned marriage issues, bearing of weapons in a church, priests exercising secular functions and holding a chieftaincy.[303] The reason for Eirik's interest might be the economical advantages for the archbishop's see which were certified by Pope Celestine III.[304]

In 1194 Sverre managed to attain the consecration of his retinue priest Martin as a new bishop of Bergen. Sverre wanted bishops to be obedient to his will instead of the Archbishop's. In 1195, at the request of the king the bishops Nikolas of Oslo, Tore of Hamar, Martin of Bergen, Páll of Skálholt, and Bjarne of the Orkneys sent a letter to Pope Celestine III complaining about disagreements between Archbishop Eirik and King Sverre.[305] The opposition between the two powers was getting more intensive. In 1195, bishop Tore of Hamar joined Archbishop Eirik in his exile in Denmark. His example was followed by bishops Njal of Stavanger and Martin of Bergen in 1197 and 1198 respectively.

What was the position of the Icelandic bishops in this conflict? On one hand, there is evidence that they took the side of the king. The bishop of Skálholt Páll was a relative of the king and was consecrated by his request.[306] Moreover, Pope Innocent III in his letter issued in 1198 warned Icelandic bishops against connections with the king.[307]

At the same time, a letter dated 1198 from the Icelandic bishops Páll of Skálholt and Brand of Hólar to Pope Innocent III (or Celestine III) denotes the opposite. Bishops gave an account of conditions in Iceland and asked for guidance and support.[308] The following correspondence between Iceland and Rome shows that the bishops tried to establish direct contacts with the Curia and abandoned supremacy of Norway. Most likely, the bishops aimed to satisfy the claims of both sides of the conflict and at the same time to make a use of one side of the conflict against the other one.

The culmination of the conflict between Sverre and the Church was the papal interdict imposed on Norway in 1198. Principal issues of the clash were: church patron rights, bishop's elections, and church jurisdiction. There were also personal disagreements between the archbishop and the king. Sverre refused to recognize a deal between Archbishop Eystein and Erling Skakke about taxes to the archbishopric in full-silver coins, and wished to cut down the archbishop's attendants from 90 to 30 persons. Eirik denied crowning Sverre without the Pope's permission.[309]

---

[303] Reg N, no. 196, 211
[304] Pope Celestine III approved privileges of Nidaros given by the previous kings: a right to send 30 *lester* of flour to Iceland and to tax one Icelandic ship each year. Source: Reg N, no. 226
[305] Reg N, no. 232
[306] Páll's grandmother, Tora, was a daughter of the Norwegian King Magnus Barefoot.
[307] DI, no. 76
[308] Reg N, no. 246
[309] Helle 1964: 59

After the death of Sverre in 1202 his son Håkon Sverreson renewed all the privileges of the Church.

What were the differences and similarities between the European pattern of the bishop's office and the Icelandic one?

Nominally the Icelandic bishops were the head of Christendom in the country. In general, Icelandic ecclesiastics followed the regulations of the Christian Church concerning the duties and rights of bishop. They consecrated churches, served the Holy Mass, performed the canonical visitation of the diocese, educated youth and trained clergy. Sources of ecclesiastical character also add bishops' care about the true faith and a high moral tone among the people. The authority to punish people by an interdict or excommunication was fully used only by Bishop Þorlákr Þórhallsson. Enactments of the Church Council were not implemented in Iceland and did not influence affairs in the Icelandic Church.

Similar to German ecclesiastics, the Icelandic ones were closely connected with the secular leaders; however, the political situation in Iceland made it possible and in some cases desirable for the most prominent secular leader to occupy the office of bishop. Unlike the German bishops the high ecclesiastics in Iceland did not exercise a key role in the administration system. Icelandic bishops were not attendants of the secular power, and, consequently were not occupied with diplomatic or managerial functions.

The development of the bishop's office in Denmark shows subordination to the royal power in the early stages and considerable transformation in the twelfth century. Danish bishops were getting more and more powerful and became a full political force. Icelandic ecclesiastics were not a detached political force.

The Norwegian pattern of the bishop's office reveals more similarities with the Icelandic one. Similar to the abovementioned instances, Norwegian bishops from the foundation of the office were under the full control of the king. However, analogous to the situation in Iceland Norwegian ecclesiastics participated at the public assembles and lawmaking processes there.[310]

The bishop's office in Germany, Denmark, and Norway in the twelfth century were at different stages of development. It was the reason for the dissimilar functions of the ecclesiastics. The supreme secular authority in the abovementioned countries used the bishops as its representatives in the public sphere. The Icelandic government system lacked the king as a top of the power hierarchy. Icelandic chieftains kept full control over the bishop's office, but did not use bishops as their representatives.

---

[310] It is not known, however, how influential they were

Conclusion:

Working on the topic of the bishops' function, I came up with the following conclusions.

All Icelandic bishops (with one exception) were a part of the Icelandic aristocratic network. On the top of this network were the chieftains – leaders of the most powerful families. The Episcopal see at Skálholt was founded by the heads of the Haukdælir family, the chieftains Ísleifr and Gizurr. The first two bishops exercised authority on the basis of their secular status. Since the basis of authority of the highest ecclesiastics was their families, the bishops' policies were held in the interests of the family.

After the death of Bishop Gizurr the bishop-chieftain pattern has changed. The office of bishop lost its significance for the heads of the Haukdælir family. Nevertheless, the see at Skálholt was under the control of the Haukdælir until 1178. All the bishops were distant relatives of the Haukdælir; they had respected, but not influential ancestry. The position of the bishops Þorlákr and Magnús was weak, since family background defined the bishops' position in the aristocratic network. These bishops tried to establish themselves in the Icelandic aristocratic milieu by traditional means: through friendship with powerful men, by gift-giving and delivering feasts.

In the middle of the twelfth century the head of the Haukdælir became interested in the bishop's office. The figure of Hallr Teitsson, a head of the family, was an attempt by the Haukdælir to come back to the bishop-chieftain pattern. This fact signifies growing importance of the bishop's office in the Skálholt diocese. The office became profitable and chieftains wished to take it under the direct control.

The 1150s marked an alteration of control over the see. Among the close friends and relatives of Bishop Klængr were the heads of the dominant families – the Haukdælir and the Oddaverjar. The successors of Klængr in office – bishops Þorlákr and Páll – were members of the Oddaverjar family. Apparently their candidatures to the see were a part of the alliance between the Haukdælir and the Oddaverjar, who had come to dominate the southern part of the country. The Haukdælir retained their influence over the see but allowed the Oddaverjar to select the bishops.[311] Bishop Þorlákr was the only bishop whose ancestry was neither influential nor respected. Þorlákr was a new type of bishop, who relied on the authority of the Catholic Church, not a family. Owing to the fact that the bishop was the first elected candidate of the Oddaverjar at Skálholt and had none of the traditional sources of authority, we can suppose that the Oddaverjar, in promoting Þorlákr to office, wished to keep it under their full control. Moreover, the Oddaverjar were dissatisfied by the policy of the northern bishop Brandr, who was the first protégé of the family in the bishop's office in Iceland. Brandr, being related to the both opponents of the feud between Sturla Þórðarson and Einarr Þorgilsson, at first backed Sturla against the Oddaverjar party. However, the hopes of the Oddaverjar concerning Þorlákr failed.

---

[311] Órri Vésteinsson 1996: 159

His episcopate became troublesome for the Icelandic chieftains. Bishop Þorlákr lacking power of the family as a basis for his own influence, started to rely on the authority of the Church and became an opponent of the Oddaverjar. The successor of Þorlákr, Bishop Páll, was a return to the bishop-chieftain pattern. Being an illegitimate son of the head of the Oddaverjar, Páll was well established in the aristocratic network of Iceland and protected the interests of his family.

The situation in the northern bishopric was different. All the Hólar bishops, except Bishop Jón, were members of the local powerful families – the Svínfellingar and the Húnröðlingar and the chieftains by rank. However, none of them belonged to the dominant family of Skagafjörður – the Ásbirnings. All the northern bishops studied on the South and/or were connected by family ties with the leaders of the South – the Haukdælir or the Oddaverjar – who obviously did not want to loose control over the North. The Oddaverjar drove the Haukdælir from the Northern bishopric in the middle of the twelfth century. Their candidate was Bishop Brandr, who came from the local powerful family, which was a side-branch of the Oddaverjar.

The Icelandic pattern of the bishops' election until the second half of the twelfth century is not very clear. One of the reasons is a source problem. Nevertheless, it is known that Icelandic bishops were not elected by the cathedral chapters because of the absence of them in Iceland. The selection of bishops of the Skálaholt bishopric was in the hands of the Haukdælir family. The method of the selection is not known; however, all the candidates were either members of Haukdælir family or controlled by them. Other families were either not powerful enough to propose their candidates or were not interested in the bishop's office.

Selection and consecration of the northern bishops was influenced at first by the Haukdælir and later by the Oddaverjar families. The appointment of St. Jón, who was a foster son of Bishop Gizurr, to the see at Hólar was an attempt by the Haukdælir to establish direct control over the North. Although succeeding bishops were members of the local powerful families – the Svínfellingar and the Húnröðlingar – they were linked with the Haukdælir, and from the second half of the twelfth century with the Oddaverjar. Election of Bishop Ketill is a single instance of the direct appointment to the Episcopal office by a chieftain.

Usually a bishop was selected after the death of his forebear in office. Yet, there are two instances when Icelandic bishops asked the archbishop to consecrate or to name his successor before his (the bishop's) death. Habitually, the bishops approved a candidacy for the bishop-elect of the second see. Sources, until the second half of the twelfth century, when talking about elections, mention only a single candidate. After the elections, a bishop-elect with a letter and the seal of an existing bishop went to the archbishopric (from 1056 to Hamburg-Bremen, from 1104 to Lund) for the consecration. Besides the consecration journey to the archbishopric some souces claim that the first bishops travelled to Rome. It seems unlikely, buut there are no means to verify this information. However, accounts about trips to Rome were the manifestation of bishops's high status and pointed on the highest authority for the Icelandic clergy.

The archbishops of Hamburg-Bremen and Lund did not have much interest in the Icelandic Church and, therefore, did not attempt to influence the elections of its leaders. A change of the archbishopric did not bring any alterations to the bishops' office.

With the foundation of the Norwegian archbishopric (1152/53)[312] Icelandic bishops went for consecration to Nidaros. Episcopal elections became an important issue from the second part of the twelfth century It was connected with the increase of influence of other powerful families – the Oddaverjar. Three candidates were named for the Skálaholt see in 1174. The consecration of the Icelandic bishop became a card played in the war of *regnum* and *sacerdotium* in Norway.

Interestingly, even as suffragants of the archdioceses in Denmark and Germany, Icelandic bishops habitually visited Norwegian royal court on their consecration journey. Contacts with Norwegian kings but not with the archbishops were underlined in the sources.

As a part of the aristocratic network of the island the bishops participated in the major conflicts of the country and so, were also players in the political game in Iceland. The study above has showed that partaking of bishops was equal in arbitration and mediation, and altogether their contribution to peacemaking concerned only significant cases, the feuds of the most powerful chieftains. Chieftains and their way of solving disputes was a role model for bishops. Intelligence, wisdom, and knowledge of law were the keystones of success in mediation/arbitration. A family determined the bishop's place in the Icelandic aristocratic network and ensured him with the means of influence. Consequently, the interests of the family determined the bishops' activities in the political game. Until the Gregorian movement started to make an impact on the Icelandic clergy and until clergy appeared who relied on authority of the Church, the bishops had no means to increase their power except traditional ones: that is the authority of a family, feasts, gifts, personal skills, and alliances with mighty men. The highest ecclesiastics took part in mediation/arbitration only when related to the main participants. I would like to underline that considering the length of the period and frequency of disputes the percentage of bishops participating in disputes was exceedingly small. Indeed, in field of peacemaking the Christian model of bishop and the Icelandic model of chieftain coincided; bishops were supposed to bring reconciliation and keep peace. Nevertheless, in Icelandic political conditions only bishops of chieftainly rank were successful in mediation and arbitration. Icelandic chieftains could accept advice

---

[312] The traditional date of the establishment of the Norwegian archdiocese is 1152/53. Obviously, the newly founded office could not start to function effectively the same year. For this reason in 1152 the bishop of Skálholt, Klængr, usually went on his consecration journey to Lund. The rest of the Icelandic bishops consecrated after Klængr went to the Nidaros archbishopric

or decisions only from persons of the same rank; otherwise, chieftains would loose their prestige. Successful intervention to the conflict led to honour and prestige for participants.[313] Comparison between the successful and failed mediation demonstrates that the first one was delivered in the frames of Icelandic legal tradition, and the second one was based on arguments of Christian obedience. Obviously, the authority of the Apostle Peter and Pope Clement IV was meaningless in the milieu of the Icelandic chieftains. The most successful and authoritative in conflicts were the bishops of chieftainly rank due to access to their traditional sources of authority – mainly power and connections of the family.

Both types of bishops could cause conflicts only in the ecclesiastical sphere. It occurred partly because the office was fixed and lifelong, so there was no need to fight for supporters and represent their interests, as did the chieftains. Moreover, Christianity provided bishops with a new kind of authority, based on the spiritual power of the Church, the Popes, and the Apostles; and gave them the potential to cause conflicts. Bishop-chieftains had traditional sources of authority and brought the Gregorian reforms into play much more rarely than Bishop Þorlákr. Brandr and Páll used a new trend for personal benefits and as a concession to the archbishop's policy. Bishop Þorlákr lacked any authority other than that of the Church. He made attempts to gain influence in fields extremely significant for the power of chieftains.

Nothing signifies that Canon Law was implemented in Iceland. Attempts to separate clerical jurisdiction from secular ones and to subordinate the Icelandic clergy to the regulations of the Catholic Church in practice, took place towards the end of the twelfth century and occurred under the pressure of the Nidaros archbishop. Under the initiative of the bishops the Christian Law section of *Grágás* were written. As for bishop's rights and duties *Grágás* concerns only the basic issues and does not indicate much about Episcopal authority. However, this legislative activity signalled the power of the bishop and was meaningful for the chieftains who used the same means to draw a line between them and society.[314]

Knowledge of laws was highly respected in Iceland. It marked one's position in society. For chieftains, training in law was important due to their activity in prosecuting and defending claims on behalf of their supporters. The bishops, knowledgeable in laws and capable in speeches were highly praised in sources. However, only on one occasion did the bishops create and implement a law – the Tithe Law. Writing down the Christian Law section should be seen in the light of the transmission from an oral to a written legal culture. The codification of the Christian laws was closely connected to

---

[313] Andersson and Miller 1989: 30
[314] Jón Viðar Sigurðsson 1999: 177

the recording of the secular laws and particularly attempts of Hafliði Másson to monopolize legislation.

Teaching and education was tremendously respected in Iceland. The secular-ecclesiastical circle of Iceland was interested in knowledge (both Christian and the traditional one). Education was one of the bishops' duties. The Skálholt and Hólar Schools, which were headed by bishops, were important centres of learning where the traditional pattern of oral transmission of knowledge was combined with the Christian one based on a book. In Iceland secular and religious teaching was not separated as it was in Europe. The schools at the sees were not the only educational centres in Iceland; there were the so-called secular schools at Haukdælir and Oddi.

Until the middle of the twelfth century the Gregorian reform did not reach Iceland. The liberation (juridical) of ecclesiastical elections from secular influence was on the agenda of the Catholic Church since the eleventh century. The popes of the second half of the twelfth century were particularly active in the reinforcement of the Church as an organization. The rights and privileges of the Pope and, thus, the archbishops, were expanded.

For the Norwegian archbishop control over the Icelandic Church was a matter of prestige and economical advantages. The requests of Archbishop Eystein towards Iceland concerned the main issues on the agenda of the Catholic Church: marriage and promiscuity matters, injustice and violence against clerics, lay investiture, duties and the conduct of clergy. Bishop Þorlákr became a supporter of the archbishop's policy in Iceland and a promoter of the Gregorian reform. In his campaign Þorlákr concentrated on marriage, concubinage, and possession of church issues.[315]

The Icelandic practise of concubinage was not specific or unusual for the Church. In Europe lay concubinage persisted through the Middle Ages. The Church did not finally and definitely prohibit concubinage among the laity until the Reformation period.[316] Interference into matrimonial affairs in Iceland as everywhere else in Europe gave the Church considerable political influence. Moreover, the supreme authority of ecclesiastics in this issue made it possible for it to have an impact on many other important issues – such as property, alliances and power.

Problems of the Þorlákr's campaign concerning church property and possession of the churches were discussed above. Þorlákr was fighting against concubinage in vain. The chieftains did not obey his orders. Archbishop Eystein could not support his adherent any more due to the complex political circumstances.[317] King Sverre Sigurdsson strove to recover control over the election of bishops and

---

[315] Well-established bishops Brandr and Páll also raised questions of marriage, promiscuity, and church property; however, for the bishops these cases were means to gain personal benefits, but not liberties for the Church.
[316] Brundage 1975: 10
[317] Such as Sverre's revolt; Eystein's exile to England.

ecclesiastical property. In the conflict between the king and the archbishop, the Icelandic bishops aimed to satisfy the claims of both sides and at the same time to use one side of the conflict against the other one.

What characteristics could be given to the Icelandic Church? Until the middle of the eleventh century there was no organized Church in Iceland. Although various regulations were gradually introduced prescribing Christian customs such as fasting and observance of the Sabbath and the feasts of the Church calendar, no ecclesiastical law was implemented until the twelfth century.[318] Unlike the Christian institutions in Europe the early Icelandic Church did not become a state within the state and kept a close symbiosis with secular power circles.

Jóhannesson emphasizes English influence on ecclesiastical situation in Iceland during the first half of the eleventh century.[319] Lárusson underlines the continental one.[320] Almost certainly, it is not possible to define which one was dominant. Most of the priests were definitely foreigners. The Church system looks like Germanic *Eigenkirche*, where the owner of the farm outs up a church at his own expense and donates a part of the farm in bond to ensure the upkeep of the church, but reserves that part for his own use as long as he fulfils his duties as church-owner.[321]

---

[318] Jón Jóhannesson 1974: 140, 143
[319] Ibid., p. 140
[320] Magnús Már Lárusson 1965: 106–7
[321] Ibid.

Abbreviations:

DI	Diplomatarium Islandicum
Grg I	Grágás I
Grg II	Grágás II
Lat Doc	Latinske documenter til norsk historie
KLNM	Kulturhistorisk leksikon for nordisk middelalder fra vikingetid til reformationstid
Ps	Páls saga
Reg N	Regesta Norvegica
Gsb	Guðmundar saga biskups
Gsd	Guðmundar saga dýra
HSs	Hvamm-Sturla saga
Ís	Íslendingasaga
Jsh	Jóns saga helga
Js Gunnlaug	Jóns biskups saga eptir Gunnlaug múnk
Þs A	Þorláks saga A
Þs B	Þorláks saga B
ÞsH	Þorgils saga ok Hafliða

Appendices:

Appendix 1: Genealogical tables

A. Bishops of the Haukdælir family
    (based on *Biskupa sögur* 2000, CLVI)

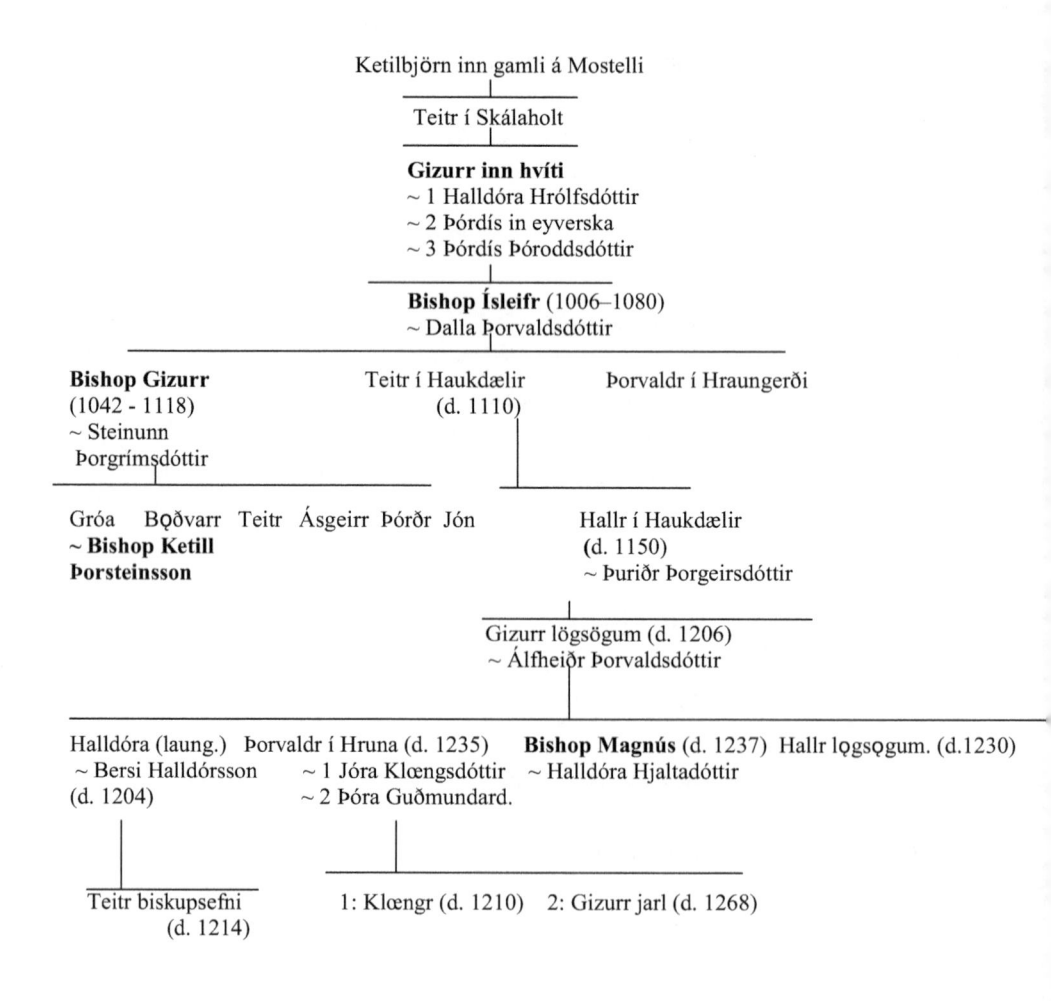

```
                        Ketilbjörn inn gamli á Mostelli
                                    |
                            Teitr í Skálaholt
                                    |
                            Gizurr inn hvíti
                            ~ 1 Halldóra Hrólfsdóttir
                            ~ 2 Þórdís in eyverska
                            ~ 3 Þórdís Þóroddsdóttir
                                    |
                            Bishop Ísleifr (1006–1080)
                            ~ Dalla Þorvaldsdóttir
```

Bishop Gizurr   Teitr í Haukdælir   Þorvaldr í Hraungerði
(1042 - 1118)   (d. 1110)
~ Steinunn
  Þorgrímsdóttir

Gróa Bǫðvarr Teitr Ásgeirr Þórðr Jón   Hallr í Haukdælir
~ Bishop Ketill   (d. 1150)
Þorsteinsson   ~ Þuríðr Þorgeirsdóttir

                            Gizurr lögsögum (d. 1206)
                            ~ Álfheiðr Þorvaldsdóttir

Halldóra (laung.) Þorvaldr í Hruna (d. 1235) **Bishop Magnús** (d. 1237) Hallr lǫgsǫgum. (d.1230)
~ Bersi Halldórsson ~ 1 Jóra Klœngsdóttir   ~ Halldóra Hjaltadóttir
(d. 1204)   ~ 2 Þóra Guðmundard.

Teitr biskupsefni   1: Klœngr (d. 1210)   2: Gizurr jarl (d. 1268)
   (d. 1214)

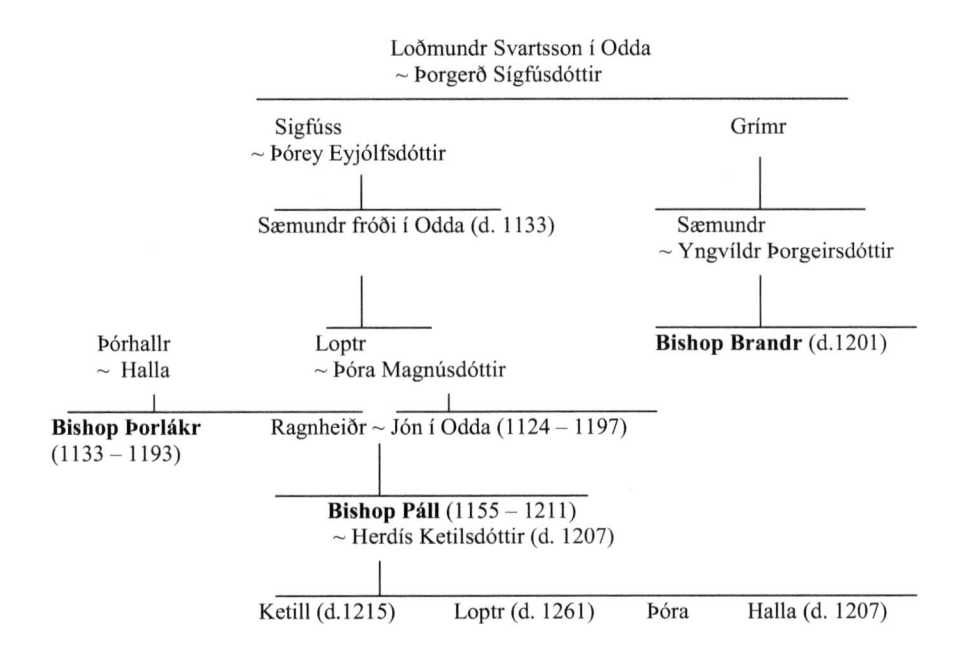

B. Bishops of the Oddaverjar family
(based on *Biskupa sögur* 2000, CLV)

```
                        Loðmundr Svartsson í Odda
                        ~ Þorgerð Sígfúsdóttir
            ┌───────────────────────┬───────────────────────┐
            Sigfúss                                         Grímr
            ~ Þórey Eyjólfsdóttir                            │
            │                                                │
            Sæmundr fróði í Odda (d. 1133)                  Sæmundr
                                                            ~ Yngvíldr Þorgeirsdóttir
                                                             │
  Þórhallr      Loptr                                        Bishop Brandr (d.1201)
  ~ Halla       ~ Þóra Magnúsdóttir
    │             │
  Bishop Þorlákr  Ragnheiðr ~ Jón í Odda (1124 – 1197)
  (1133 – 1193)              │
                            Bishop Páll (1155 – 1211)
                            ~ Herdís Ketilsdóttir (d. 1207)
                             │
            ┌────────────┬───────────┬──────────┐
         Ketill (d.1215)  Loptr (d. 1261)  Þóra  Halla (d. 1207)
```

C. Linage of Niðjar Þorfinns karlsefnis
(based on *Biskupa sögur* 2000, CLVII)

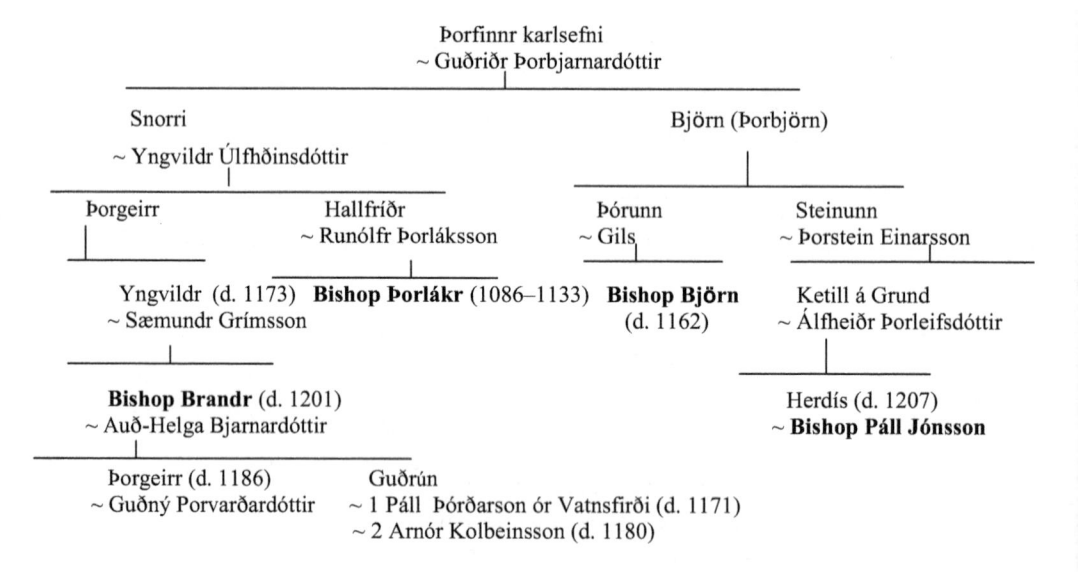

Þorfinnr karlsefni
~ Guðríðr Þorbjarnardóttir

Snorri
~ Yngvildr Úlfhðinsdóttir

Björn (Þorbjörn)

Þorgeirr

Hallfríðr
~ Runólfr Þorláksson

Þórunn
~ Gils

Steinunn
~ Þorstein Einarsson

Yngvildr (d. 1173) **Bishop Þorlákr** (1086–1133) **Bishop Björn** Ketill á Grund
~ Sæmundr Grímsson   (d. 1162)   ~ Álfheiðr Þorleifsdóttir

Bishop Brandr (d. 1201)   Herdís (d. 1207)
~ Auð-Helga Bjarnardóttir   ~ **Bishop Páll Jónsson**

Þorgeirr (d. 1186)   Guðrún
~ Guðný Þorvarðardóttir   ~ 1 Páll Þórðarson ór Vatnsfirði (d. 1171)
                          ~ 2 Arnór Kolbeinsson (d. 1180)

D. **Linage of the Síðumenn**
(based on *Biskupa sögur* 2000, CLVIII)

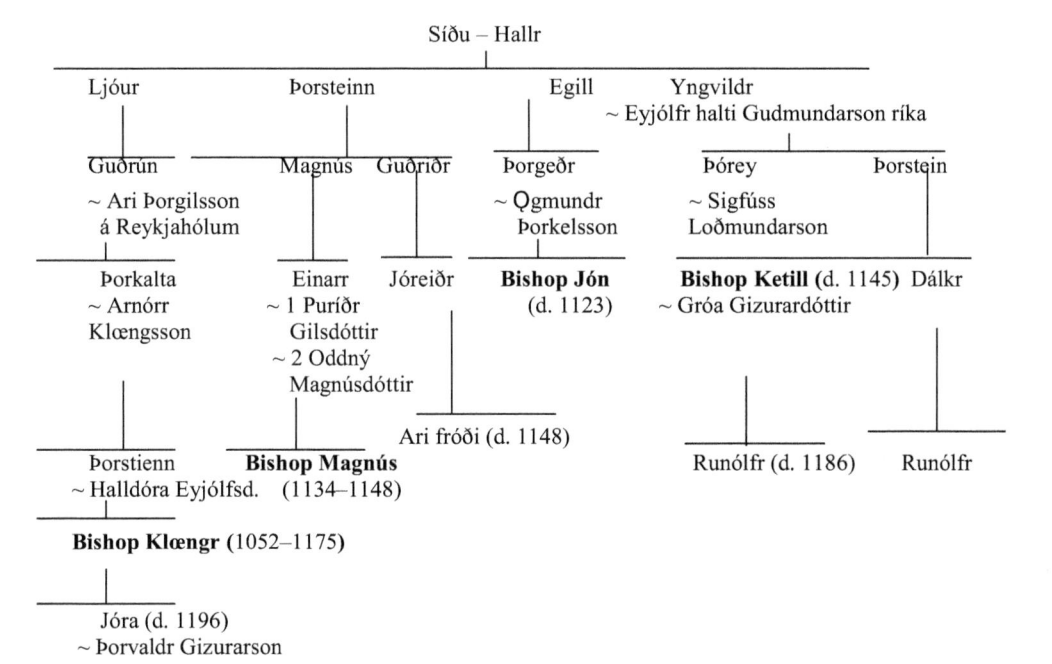

```
                                    Síðu – Hallr
    ┌───────────────┬───────────────────┬──────────────────────┐
  Ljóur         Þorsteinn             Egill                Yngvildr
    │               │                    │          ~ Eyjólfr halti Gudmundarson ríka
    │               │                    │                    │
  Guðrún      Magnús  Guðríðr       Þorgeðr            Þórey        Þorstein
 ~ Ari Þorgilsson                ~ Ǫgmundr          ~ Sigfúss
  á Reykjahólum                   Þorkelsson       Loðmundarson
    │               │                    │                    │
  Þorkalta     Einarr    Jóreiðr    Bishop Jón     Bishop Ketill (d. 1145)   Dálkr
  ~ Arnórr    ~ 1 Puríðr              (d. 1123)    ~ Gróa Gizurardóttir
   Klœngsson    Gilsdóttir
              ~ 2 Oddný
               Magnúsdóttir
                            Ari fróði (d. 1148)
    │               │                                         │
  Þorstienn   Bishop Magnús                         Runólfr (d. 1186)    Runólfr
  ~ Halldóra Eyjólfsd.  (1134–1148)
    │
  Bishop Klœngr (1052–1175)
    │
   Jóra (d. 1196)
  ~ Þorvaldr Gizurarson
```

Appendix 2: Lists of ecclesiastical succession

A. Icelandic bishops (1056 – 1211)
(based on Jón Jóhannesson 1974, p. 369)

Skalholt bishopric

Ísleifr Gizurarson	1056 – 1080
Gizurr Ísleifsson	1082 – 1118
Þorlákr Runólfsson	1118 – 1133
Magnús Einarsson	1134 – 1148
bishop-elect Hallr Teitsson	d. 1148
Klængr Þorsteinsson	1152 – 1176
Þorlákr Þórhallsson	1178 – 1193
Páll Jónsson	1195 – 1211

Hólar bishopric

Jón Ögmundson	1106 – 1121
Ketill Þorsteinsson	122 – 1145
Björn Gilsson	1147 – 1162
Brandr Sæmundson	1163 – 1201

B.   Archbishops of Hamburg-Bremen (1043 – 1104)
(based on www.newadvent.org)

Adalbert the Great	1043-72
Liemar	1072-1101
Humbert	1101-04

C.   Archbishops of Lund (1104 – 1152/53)
(based on www.newadvent.org)

Özurr (Azzur, Aserus)	1104 – 1136
Eskill	1137 – 1177

D.   Archbishops of Nidaros (1153/54 – 1214)
(based on www.newadvent.org)

Jón Birgisson	app.1154 – 1157
Eystein Erlendsson	1160/61 – 1188
Eirik Ivarsson	1189 – 1206
Tore	1206 – 1214

E.   Popes (1055 – 1216)
(based on www.newadvent.org)

Victor	1055 – 1057	Celestine II	1143 – 1144
Stephen X	1057 – 1058	Lucius II	1144 – 1145
Nicholas II	1058 – 1061	Blessed Eugene III	1145 – 1153
Alexander II	1061 – 1073	Anastasius IV	1153 – 1154
St. Gregory VII	1073 – 1085	Adrian IV	1154 – 1159
Blessed Victor III	1086 – 1087	Alexander III	1159 – 1181
Blessed Urban II	1088 – 1099	Lucius III	1181 – 1185
Paschal II	1099 – 1118	Urban III	1185 – 1187
Gelasius II	1118 – 1119	Gregory VIII	1187
Callistus II	1119 – 1124	Clement III	1187 – 1191

Honorius II	1124 – 1130	Celestine III	1191 – 1198
Innocent II	1130 – 1143	Innocent III	1198 – 1216

Bibliography:

Primary sources

Diplomatarium Islandicum, Íslenzkt forbréfasafn I. Jón Sigurðsson a.o. Copenhagen and Reykjavik.1857 – 76.

Grágás. Laws of Early Iceland I – II. Trans. A. Dennis, P. Foote, and R. Perkins. Winnipeg 1980.

Hungrvaka. *Biskupa sögur* II. Ed. Jónas Kristjánsson. Reykjavík 2000.

Hungrvaka. *Origines Islandicae: a collection of the more important sagas and other nativewritings relating to the settlement and early history of Iceland.* Trans. G. Vigfusson and F. Y. Powell. Oxford 1905.

Jóns biskups saga, eptir Gunnlaug múnk. *Biskupa sögur* I. Guðbrandur Vigfússon. København 1858.

Latinske dokument til norsk historie fram til ar 1204. Ed. E. Vandvik. Oslo 1959.

Páls saga. *Biskupa sögur* II. Ed. Jónas Kristjánsson. Reykjavík 2000.

Póls saga. *Origines Islandicae: a collection of the more important sagas and other nativewritings relating to the settlement and early history of Iceland.* Trans. G. Vigfusson and F. Y. Powell. Oxford 1905.

Regesta Norvegica, I. 822 – 1263. Ed. E. Gunnes. Oslo 1989.

Saga of bishop Jón of Hólar. *Medieval hagiography: an anthology.* Ed. Thomas Head. Trans. by Margaret Cormack. New York 2001.

Saga of Guðmund Arason the priest. *Sturlunga saga* II. Trans. J. H. McGrew and R G. Thomas. New York 1970.

Saga of Guðmundr dýri. *Sturlunga saga* II. Trans. J. H. McGrew and R G. Thomas. New York 1970.

Saga of Hvamm-Sturla. *Sturlunga saga* I. Trans. J. H. McGrew and R G. Thomas. New York 1970.

Saga Jóns biskups his elzta. *Biskupa sögur* I. Guðbrandur Vigfússon. København 1858.

Saga of Hrolf Kraki. Trans. by Stella M. Mills. Oxford 1933.

Saga of the Icelanders. *Sturlunga saga* I. Trans. J.H. McGrew. New York 1970.

Saxo Grammaticus. Danmarks Krønike. Oversat af Fr. Winkel Horn. Sesam 1994.

Snorri Sturluson. Heimskringla. History of the Kings of Norway. Trans. by L. M. Hollander. Austin, Tex. 1995.

Sturla Þórðarson. Íslendingasaga. Trans. by A. V. Zimmerling. Sankt-Petersburg 2007. (In rus.: Стурла Тордарсон. Сага об исландцах. Пер. и коммент. Циммерлинга А.В. Санкт-Петербург 2007)

The Tale of the Men of Haukadal. *Sturlunga saga* II. Trans. J. H. McGrew and R G. Thomas. New York 1970.

Þorláks saga A. *Biskupa sögur* II. Ed. Jónas Kristjánsson. Reykjavík 2000.

Þorláks saga. *Origines Islandicae: a collection of the more important sagas and other nativewritings relating to the settlement and early history of Iceland.* Trans. G. Vigfusson and F. Y. Powell. Oxford 1905.

Þorláks saga B. *Biskupa sögur* II. Ed. Jónas Kristjánsson. Reykjavík 2000.

Oddaverja-þáttr. *Origines Islandicae: a collection of the more important sagas and other nativewritings relating to the settlement and early history of Iceland.* Trans. G. Vigfusson and F. Y. Powell. Oxford 1905.

Þorgils saga ok Hafliða. *Sturlunga saga* II. Trans. J. H. McGrew and R G. Thomas. New York 1970.

Secondary sources

Addleshaw, G.W.O. 1956, Rectors, vicars and patrons in twelfth and early thirteenth century canon law. York.

Andersson, T.M. and Miller, W. I. 1989, Preface. *Ljósvetninga saga and Valla-Ljóts saga. Law and literature in Medieval Iceland.* Stanford, vii - xiii.

Arnold, B. 2004, "The western empire, 1125 – 1197." *The New Cambridge Medieval History*, IV (2). Eds. D. Luscombe and J. Riley-Smith. Cambridge, 384–421.

Ásdís Egilsdóttir. 1992, "Eru biskupasögur til?" Skáldskaparmál, 2, 207–20.

Bagge, S. 2003, "Den heroiske tid – kirkereform og kirkekamp 1153–1214." *Ecclesia Nidrosiensis 1153–1537.* Ed. Steinar Imsen. Oslo, 51–81.

Barraclough, G. 1934, "The Making of a Bishop in the Middle Ages." The Catholic Historical Review, 19, 275–319.

Bekker-Nielsen, H. 1972, "Hungrvaka and the medieval Icelandic Audience." Studi Germanici, 10, 94– 8.

Benson, Robert L. 1968, The bishop-elect: a study in medieval ecclesiastical office. Princeton.

Blom, G.A. 1967, Kongemakt og privilegier i Norge inntil 1387. Oslo.

Blumenthal, U. R. 2004, "The papacy, 1024–1122." *The New Cambridge Medieval History*, IV (2). Eds. D. Luscombe and J. Riley-Smith. Cambridge, 8–38.

Bourchard, Counstance Brittain. 2004, "The bishop as aristocrat: the case of Hugh of Chalon." *The bishop: power and piety at the first millennium.* Ed. S. Gilsdorf. Münster, 37–50.

Brooke, Z.N. 1989, The English church and the papacy. Cambridge.

Brundage, James A. 1975, "Concubinage and marriage in medieval canon law." Journal of medieval history, 1 (1), 1–18.

Burton, J. 1995, Monastic and religious orders in Britain, 1000–1300. Cambridge.

Byock, J. L. 1982, Feud in the Icelandic Saga. Berkeley.

- 1985, "Cultural continuity, the Church, and the concept of Independent Ages in Medieval Iceland." Skandinavistik, 13 (2), 1–14.

- 1988, Medieval Iceland. Society, Sagas, and Power. Berkeley.

Duby, Georges. 1997–8, *Women of the Twelfth century*, I. Cambridge.

Foote, Peter. 1984, *Aurvandilstá: Norse studies*. The Viking Collection 2. Odense.

Gilsdorf, S. 2004, "Bishops in the Middle: mediatory politics and the episcopacy." *The bishop: power and piety at the first millennium*. Ed. S. Gilsdorf. Münster, 51–74.

Gunnes, E. 1996, Erkebiskop Øystein : statsmann og kirkebygger. Oslo.

Gurevich, A. J. 1984, Categories of medieval culture. Moscow. (In rus: Гуревич А.Я. Категории средневековой культуры. Москва 1984)

Gísli Sigurðsson. 2004, The medieval Icelandic saga and oral tradition: a discourse on method. Cambridge.

Hansen, E. M. 1999, En undersøkelse av drap, hevndrap og feide i Heimskringla og seks islendingesagaer. Hovedfag i Historie. Oslo.

Helle, K. 1964, Norge blir en stat 1130–1319. Handbok i Norges historie 3. Bergen.

Hjalti Hugason. 2000, Kristini á Íslandi I. Alþingi.

Hood, J. C. F. 1946. Icelandic Church Saga. London.

Hörður Ágústsson. 1990, Skálholt. Kirkjur. Reykjavík.

Jaeger, S. 1983, "The courtier bishop." Speculum, 58(2): 291325, 291–325.

Johnsen, A. O. 1945, Studier vedrørende kardinal Nicolaus Brekespears legasjon til Norden. Oslo.

- 1955, Bispesetet og erkestolen i Nidaros fra den eldste tid til 1252. Oslo.

- 2003, "Nidaros erkebispestol og bispestede." *Ecclesia Nidrosiensis 1153–1537*. Red. S. Imsen. Trondheim.

Joys, Ch. 1948, Biskop og konge: bispevalg i Norge 1000-1350. Oslo.

Jørgensen, J. H., 1982, "Hagiography in the Icelandic Bishop Sagas." Peritia, 1, 1–16.

Jón Helgason. 1925, Islands Kirke fra dens Grundlæggelse til Reformationen: en historisk Fremstilling. København.

Jón Jóhannesson. 1974, A history of the old Icelandic commonwealth: íslendinga saga. Winnipeg.

Jón Viðar Sigurðsson. 1999, Chieftains and power in the Icelandic commonwealth. Odense.

- 1994, "Forholdet mellom verdslig og religiøs makt på Island i fristatsperioden." *Myte og ritual i det førkristne norden*. Et symposium. Eds. J. P. Schjødt, U. Drobin. Odense, 129–140.

Jónas Kristjánsson. 1997, Eddas and Sagas. Icelandic medieval literature. Reykjavík.

Korpiola, M. 1999, "An uneasy harmony: consummation and parental consent in secular and canon law in medieval Scandinavia." *Nordic perspectives on medieval canon law*. Ed. M. Korpiola. Helsinki, 125–150.

Knowles, D. 1962, The Monastic Order in England. Cambridge.

Kulturhistorisk leksikon for nordisk middelalder fra vikingetid til reformationstid, I, V. Oslo 1956–78.

Magnús Már Lárusson.1965, "The church of Iceland." *Scandinavian churches. A picture of the development and life of the churches of Denmark, Finland, Iceland, Norway and Sweden*. Ed. L. S. Hunter. London, 104–10.

Mair, L. 1972, An introduction to social anthropology. Oxford.

Mauss, M. 1969, The gift: forms and functions of exchange in archaic societies. London.

Mc Guire, P. 1999, "Monks and their books." *Levende ord & lysende billeder : den middelalderlige bogkultur i Danmark : essays*. Ed. E. Petersen. København, 105–126.

Miller, W. I. 1990, Bloodtaking and peacemaking: feud, law, and society in Saga Iceland. Chicago and London.

Mulen, L. 2002, Everyday life of medieval monks in Western Europe, 10th – 15th ct. Moscow. (In rus: Мулен Л. Повседневная жизнь средневековых монахов Западной Европы X-XV века. Москва 2002.)

Nygård, B. M. 1997, Ok óksu allir upp heima þar. Hovudoppgåve i Historie. Bergen.

Oftestad, B. T., Rasmussen, T. and Schumacher, J. 1991, Norsk kirkehistorie. Oslo.

Olason, V. 2000, "Topography and world view in Njals saga." *Gudar på jorden*. Festskrift till Lars Lonnroth. Eds. S. Hansson, M. Malm. Stockholm, 131–142.

Órri Vésteinsson. 1996, The Christianization of Iceland: Priests, Power and Social Change 1000–1300. London.

Parisse, M. 2004, "The bishop: prince and prelate." *The bishop: power and piety at the first millennium*. Ed. S. Gilsdorf. Münster, 1–22.

Perron, A. 2003A, "Ius metropoliticum" of the Norwegian Periphery from Nicolas Brekspear to William of Sabina." Paper was presented in a session on "Legislation and the Church in Medieval Scandinavia." *At the Thirty-Eight International Congress on Medieval Studies.* Michigan.

- 2003B, "Metropolitan might and papal power on the Latin Christian frontier: transforming the Danish church around the time of the forth Lateran council." The Catholic Historical Review 89, 186–7.

Reuter, T. 2004, "Bishops, rights of passage, and the symbolism of state in pre-Gregorian Europe." *The bishop: power and piety at the first millennium.* Ed. S. Gilsdorf. Münster, 23–36.

Robinson, I.S. 1990, The papacy 1073–1198: continuity and innovation. Cambridge.

Samson, R. 1991, "Economic anthropology and Vikings." *Social approaches to Viking studies.* Ed. R. Samson. Glasgow, 87–96.

Sigurður Nordal. 1990, Icelandic culture. Cornell.

Smith, K. P. Parsons, J. R. 1989, "Regional Archaeological Research in Iceland: Potentials and Possibilities." *The Anthropology of Iceland.* Ed. E. P. Durrenberger, G. Palsson. Iowa City, 179–203.

The Oxford dictionary of the Christian Church. 1990, Eds. F.L. Cross, E.A. Livingstone. London.

Ullman, Walter. 1976, The papacy and the political ideas in the Middle Ages. London.

Vestergaard, E. 1991, "Gift-giving, hoarding, and outdoings." *Social approaches to Viking studies.* Ed. R. Samson. Glasgow, 97–105.

Wright, C.E. 1939, The cultivation of saga in Anglo-Saxon England. Edinburg.

VDM

Verlag Dr. Müller

Wissenschaftlicher Buchverlag bietet

kostenfreie

Publikation

von

wissenschaftlichen Arbeiten

Diplomarbeiten, Magisterarbeiten, Master und Bachelor Theses
sowie Dissertationen, Habilitationen und wissenschaftliche Monographien

Sie verfügen über eine wissenschaftliche Abschlußarbeit zu aktuellen oder zeitlosen Fragestellungen, die hohen inhaltlichen und formalen Ansprüchen genügt, und haben **Interesse an einer honorarvergüteten Publikation**?

Dann senden Sie bitte erste Informationen über Ihre Arbeit per Email an info@vdm-verlag.de. Unser Außenlektorat meldet sich umgehend bei Ihnen.

VDM Verlag Dr. Müller Aktiengesellschaft & Co. KG
Dudweiler Landstraße 125a
D - 66123 Saarbrücken

www.vdm-verlag.de